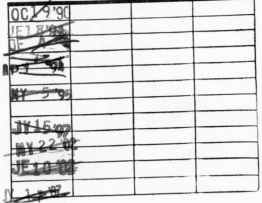

WHY MANY
COLLEGE TEACHERS
CANNOT LECTURE

WHY MANY COLLEGE TEACHERS CANNOT LECTURE

HOW TO AVOID COMMUNICATION BREAKDOWN IN THE CLASSROOM

By

JON G. PENNER, M.S., Ph.D.

Associate Professor of Speech
Lake Michigan College
Benton Harbor, Michigan

CHARLES C THOMAS • PUBLISHER

Springfield • Illinois • U.S.A.

Published and Distributed Throughout the World by
CHARLES C THOMAS • PUBLISHER
2600 South First Street
Springfield, Illinois 62717

© *1984 by* CHARLES C THOMAS • PUBLISHER
ISBN 0-398-04936-X
Library of Congress Catalog Card Number: 83-18313

With **THOMAS BOOKS** *careful attention is given to all details of manufacturing and design. It is the Publisher's desire to present books that are satisfactory as to their physical qualities and artistic possibilities and appropriate for their particular use.* THOMAS BOOKS *will be true to those laws of quality that assure a good name and good will.*

Printed in the United States of America
Q-R-3

Library of Congress Cataloging in Publication Data
Penner, Jon G. (Jonathan Gunther), 1922-
  Why many college teachers cannot lecture.

  Bibliography: p.
  Includes index.
  1. Lecture method in teaching. 2. College teaching.
3. Teacher-student   relationships.   4. Oral
communication. I. Title.
LB2393.P4 1984   378'.1796   83-18313
ISBN 0-398-04936-X

PREFACE

A number of books and many articles have been written in the field of higher education in which the weaknesses of the lecture method have been pointed out. Few of these, however, suggest that the teacher's own inadequacies and the abuses of the lecture method are very largely to blame for the ineffectiveness of the professor's presentation, as well as the general disdain of students for poor lecturing. Comparatively little has been written that deals in any way with some of the basic problems, for example, the training of teachers for lecturing, a task that consumes such a significant part of the entire teaching career. These problems include not only the rhetorical and linguistical but also the psychological aspects of classroom communication. Deficiencies in any one or in all of these areas will result in partial breakdown or total blockage of communication between teacher and student.

Poor personal qualities and a lack of training in other teaching techniques will likewise diminish effectiveness when employing such methods as discussion, seminar and tutorials.

In this book, the author endeavors to make the teachers at the college and university levels aware of these communication pitfalls, so that they might be avoided; and to direct attention to students in teacher-training programs to the obvious need of training in the communicative arts and teaching techniques, so that the ultimate aims of teaching might be realized: communicating information to the students, training them to think for themselves and inspiring them to develop intellectually and culturally to their fullest potential.

CONTENTS

WHY MANY
COLLEGE TEACHERS
CANNOT LECTURE

Part I
TEACHING AS COMMUNICATION

CHAPTER 1

TEACHING AND LEARNING
AS COMMUNICATION PROCESSES

Communication, the transmission of thought from one mind to others, is one of the basic activities of the human race — it is a skill through which men make magnificent successes and startling failures, an art without which genius is dumb, power brutal and aimless, mankind a plantload of squabbling tribes. Communication is an essential function of civilisation. Teaching is only one of the many occupations that depend upon it and depend upon it absolutely.

Gilbert Highet

THE logical place to begin a consideration of communication breakdown in college and university teaching would, first of all, be an attempt to define the purposes, aims, and objectives of higher education. Second, an effort should be made to determine in what ways teaching involves communication. Indeed, the concept of communication itself needs to be more fully explained and understood in its relationship and importance to the learning situation. Finally, one must look at the whole complex communication process and become aware of the many causes for, and results of communication barriers and breakdowns in teaching. A fuzzy perception or incorrect view of the purposes and objectives of higher education, unawareness of the complex process of communication, an inadequate training in communication skills and lack of personal qualities can plunge the teacher headlong into many pitfalls, assuring a professional lifetime of failure and ineffectual "teaching."

AIMS OF EDUCATION

The first task then is to define exactly what the teacher does when he teaches. Many attempts have been made in the past to define teaching and the aims or objectives of teaching in higher education. To arrive at such an all-inclusive specific definition is very difficult, and claimed by some as an impossibility. It has fallen my lot, on several college campuses, to serve on committees which were created solely for the purpose of determining the actual goals and objectives of teaching at that particular institution of higher learning. Enormous sums of money were expended to employ educational "experts" who conducted surveys in an effort to reach an agreement on a statement of the educational philosophy and goals of the college, so that a succinct paragraph or two could be printed on the first page of the college bulletin. So complex are the aims and purposes of higher education that no one statement or a combination of ideas could adequately depict and define the aims and objectives of higher education.

There must, however, be some common core purpose and direction to guide the teacher in training and in professional practice. From my days as graduate student at Indiana University, I recall a comprehensive definition expressed by Dr. Lee Norvelle, chairman of the Speech and Drama Department. He considered the purpose of a college education as training the student "to gather subject material which will provide a background for needs after college and to develop habits which will enable the individual to adapt himself adequately to the cultural, social, economic, spiritual, and political demands of his generation."[1]

The Hale Report of the University Grants Committee stated that "the aim of the undergraduate course . . . should be not only or even primarily to equip the student with knowledge, but also, and more importantly, to teach him to think for himself and work on his own."[2]

Not only does the effective teacher teach students to think for themselves but one might say that the good teacher does not think *for* the students but *with* them. K. G. Collier considered weaning the student from dependence on instruction and building up his or her powers of critical judgment to be one of the major problems of higher education[3].

Many years ago the American Association of University Professors issued a statement that "the purpose of college teaching is to induce self-propelled intellectual activity on the part of the student. To teach effectively is to lead, to inspire, and to guide the learner."[4] In their report, *The Importance of Teaching*, the Committee on Undergraduate Teaching outlined the ideal end results hoped for: "The ultimate result of good teaching will be found, of course, in the student — in the growth of his knowledge, the extension of his skills, the lengthening of his values, the maturing of his intellectual or creative discipline."[5]

With these definitions in mind, the process of teaching should be thought of as an activity, as suggested by John Hough and James Duran. "Teaching is an activity — a unique professional, rational, and humane activity in which one creatively and imaginatively uses himself and his knowledge to promote the learning and welfare of others. . . . Teaching is an activity with four phases — a curriculum-planning phase, an instructing phase, a measuring phase and an evaluating phase."[6] This book deals with the instructing phase of teaching. From the standpoint of the student, education is looked upon as a receiver of this teaching process and as a reactor to it. As Philip Hills expressed it, "Learning is a process of acquiring knowledge or changing attitudes, behavior or beliefs by contact with external events." He concluded that both processes — the teaching and the learning — are communicative series of actions. "Education can thus be seen as a communication process between society and the individual. . . . Education must be looked at constantly to determine how well it is communicating the standards of society and the store of man's knowledge."[7]

Since the purpose in writing this book is to point out the various ways in which communication between teacher and student in both teaching and learning processes can break down (as well as to offer suggestions how these breakdowns can be avoided or, at least, mini-mized), we need to understand what actually takes place or should take place in the various steps which comprise the total complex communication chain of events.

COMMUNICATION THEORIES

Let us take a look at the traditional communication models and then see how these theories can be adapted to the teaching situation in particular. The term *communication* comes to us from the Latin word *communicatio* through a French loan word into the English with the connotative meaning of imparting or, more accurately, that of sharing something, from which the expression *communion* is derived, as in the Eucharist, or Holy Communion. Modern definitions of this term still contain this idea of sharing or imparting. Today we say that communication is the transmission of ideas from mind to mind, or it is the process by which one person influences another.

The following is a brief review of the steps in the traditional com-munication theory as outlined by Alan Monroe.[8] First of all, it is as-sumed that the speaker thinks; as a result of which he has an idea, thought or concept in his own mind. His whole personality responds intellectually and emotionally to this thought. Second, the speaker translates his ideas into the most appropriate word symbols. This verbalization takes place instantly. Some authorities claim that we cannot think without the use of these word symbols. In the third step of communication, the speaker's brain sends neural messages to the various parts of the vocal mechanism. Forty-two pairs of muscles co-operate in the four phases of the production of speech — respiration, vibration, resonation, and articulation in vocalizing the audible rep-resentations of the word symbols. At the same time, during the voca-lization of these ideas, nonverbal messages accompany the verbal such as changes in inflection, rate, volume and voice quality. In fact, the entire body becomes involved, adding yet a third set of messages to those of the actual word symbols and the interpretation given by the vocal variety — nonverbal messages through gestures, eye con-tact, facial expressions, posture and bodily movement.

Fourthly, the listener hears and sees these messages and signals, and his eyes and ears capture the light patterns and sound vibrations and conveys them through the nerves to the brain. In the fifth step of communication, the listener decodes and interprets these visible and audible messages or signals. As a result his entire body reacts, intellectually and emotionally.

The communication process does not end here, because genuine communication is not a one-way transmission of an idea from the source to the receiver. In the sixth step, the speaker must carefully read the nonverbal (and at times verbal) reactions of the listeners and must be aware of what might be going on in the minds of the hearers. Communication must be a two-way process, and as the speaker interprets the reactions of the listeners, he responds to their expressions of doubt, disbelief, fear, disappointment or acceptance. In a single fifty-minute class period of lecturing, more than eight thousand word symobls are employed by the lecturer, and hopefully, instantly decoded by the students. At the same time there are hundreds of additional nonverbal audible and visible signs of voice and body sent out and interpreted in this rapid and complex process of communication. This complexity of the symbolic process will be further discussed in the chapter dealing with semantics and language barriers.

The six ingredients in Berlo's model of the communication process are (1) The communication source — a person or group of people with a purpose or reason for engaging in communication, (2) The message — translating ideas, purposes and intentions into a code or systematic set of symbols, (3) The encoder — via language expressing code in message, (4) The channel — the medium or carrier of the message, (5) The decoder — sensory skills or senses. As a source needs an encoder to translate his purpose into a message and express purposes in a code, the receiver must have a decoder to retranslate or to decode the message and put it into a form that the receiver can use, (6) The communication receiver — the person or persons with whom the communication is intended, who reacts or responds.[9]

Shannon and Weaver have developed a similar communication model consisting of input, coding channel, decoding and output.[10] The teacher supplies the input and coding, communicating the subject material through symbols. The channel of communication is comprised of the means by which the teacher conveys the ideas, concepts, thoughts and statements to the students — his voice, body, visual aids, including the blackboard, and audio and audiovisual devices. The students then decode the messages and produce output in note taking or discussions, examinations, or simply modified student behavior and practical application of knowledge received.

There are several general areas in which one can look for possible points of breakdown in communication from teacher to student. Some of these areas relate to the *psychological* and *ethical*, such as the students' unfavorable perception of the teacher's knowledge and ability, or personality and sincerity. The teacher may also be responsible for disrupting the communication process in the area of the *logical* in not following correct lines of argument or in the lack of clarity and arrangement of thought patterns. The stress that results when a person is confronted with that which he cannot logically follow and understand can actually be measured. Another area of disturbance to a clear flow of communication concerns the *linguistical* that results from inadequate or inaccurate vocabulary or word choice, creating in the mind of the student incomplete or incorrect meaning to language symbols. Communication barriers may also be inherent in the physical or *physiological* matters involving structural deficiencies, poor acoustics, or inappropriate volume and faults in articulation and pronunciation.

In this book, many of these factors influencing the effectiveness of the classroom communication will be dealt with in the following areas: (1) The teacher — training and education, reputation, personality and dedication; (2) the content of subject matter — organization, word choice, interest, method or technique, delivery and motivation; (3) the students — listening skills, feedback and attitudes; and (4) the environment and "climate" in which the message is given and received. Throughout this complex process of classroom communication there lurk many potential intellectual, psychological, sociological, physiological and linguistical barriers, any one or all of which could result in a partial or complete communication breakdown between the teacher and student.

COMMUNICATION IN TEACHING AND LEARNING

It is no great discovery to find that practically all learning on the college and university levels centers in the communication of knowledge in one way or another. In fact, almost all learning from the cradle to the grave takes place through some type of communication — principally language symbols. Symbols in language are not natural signs, but rather they are artificial, invented forms that do not necessarily have any connection with the object for which they stand. The value of these symbols is in their meaning which is arbitrarily decided upon by those cultures using them.

We were not born with a knowledge of these symbols, but inherited the potential ability to transform our experiences and thoughts into words. We have been told that a person cannot conceive of an idea (or think), or store up experience and knowledge without first symbolizing it in the mind. We cannot, consequently, communicate our concepts and share with others our experience and knowledge without using symbols, primarily language signs. Without language we could not reason or plan, remember or imagine, nor could we understand the meaning of life or the universe about us, or aspire, dream and hope for the future. All that man knows about science and technology, religion and philosophy, art and literature, has been acquired through the communication process. Great minds of the past have symbolized their experiences, illuminations and knowledge into language symbols, and so, likewise, teachers of today are responsible for passing on these achievements to the younger generation.

(At first we cried in order to communicate that we were angry, hungry or uncomfortable. Then one day in our vocal play when putting our lips together quickly, followed by an uninterrupted flow of air, we made the vowel sound "ah," accidentally producing our first word, "mama," and were delighted at the great deal of fuss which our mother made over us, and after that experience we put forth a more conscious effort to produce that same sequence of noises or sounds bringing about another adult reaction. The same thing happened a little later when we put together a repetition of the consonantal sound "d" quickly followed by another open vowel sound, and "dada" became the symbol for a male figure, and eventually stood for a specific male. Little by little we got the idea that everything has a name. The process of symbolization had begun in our lives and we have never been the same again since we made that discovery. From that day until now, whatever we have learned and perceived, has come to us through the vehicle of language.)

Someone estimated that the average person speaks 30,000 words a day. If we add to this sum, the amount of language symbols employed each day in such activities, as reading, listening and thinking, a person utilizes 100,000 word symbols each day. This is not to imply that the sole responsibility of the teacher is to simply repeat word symbols expressing facts or information in the act of transferring them on to the students. We have often heard it said that lecturing is the process of transferring information from the notes of the professor to the notes of the student without going through the mind of either. This notion has been expressed in various forms throughout the years. A slightly more refined version puts it this way: "The lecture system is the most reliable method by which to move knowledge from the professor's notes to a student's notes with the least mental activity generated by the passage on either side." (More about the lecture method will be discussed in later chapters.)

Communication in teaching involves the intellectual, ethical, emotional and physical powers of the instructor, as well as the activity of the listener as the student receives the communication and acts upon it. In fact, no communication really takes place without this activity of the recipient. John Dewey made the following observation concerning the transfer of ideas and knowledge from one person to another:

> No thought, no idea, can possibly be conveyed as an idea from one person to another. . . . The communication may stimulate the other person to realize the question for himself and to think out a like idea. . . Meaning emerges, thought and experiences are connected.[11]

Commenting on Dewey's view, R. S. Peters stated, "What makes difficult the transmission of ideas by communication is precisely that the process of connection cannot be achieved by the communication itself, but only by the activity of the recipient goaded by the communication."[12]

METHODS OF TEACHING

Four methods or techniques of classroom communication will be referred to in the following chapters. The first method is lecturing. The lecture method has a long history as the main technique of college and university instruction and continues to be widely used at the present time. In fact, it is still the chief means of communication in college and university classrooms today. The lecture has been defined by the Robbins Committee as a teaching period "occupied wholly or mainly with *continuous exposition by the lecturer.*"[13] There may be some limited opportunity for questions, but in general the students listen and take notes on what is being said. In a memorandum to the new college teacher, the Committee on Undergaduate Teaching suggested several variations within the lecture method. "Lecturing varies along a continuum from formal to informal, the most formal consisting of the memorized address and the read paper . . . the formal lecture, the highly organized, uninterrupted speech by the professor, usually from notes, continues to hold an important place in higher education, especially in large classes."[14] The more informal lecture, however, allows interruptions for the purpose of asking questions and students' comments. The Robbins Committee report stated that students in colleges in England and Wales spent on an average approximately sixteen hours per week in teaching periods composed of the following: lectures, 8.8 hours; seminars, 2 hours; tutorials, .1 hour; practicals, 4.8 hours and miscellaneous, .5 hour per week.

For many years much criticism has been launched against the lecture method. It has been ridiculed, caricatured, condemned and even revolted against. In the following chapters, it is the intent of the author to point out the inconsistencies and absurdities of much of this criticism. (To a lesser extent this applies also to some of the complaints about the way discussions and seminars are conducted). If the barriers to communication could be eliminated or minimized, many of the arguments put forth in the above areas, especially that of the lecture method, would vanish. Rather than condemning a particular method of teaching technique, and relegating it to obsolescence and inefficiency, even worthlessness, we need carefully to examine the causes of inefficiency and be willing to bring about the necessary changes in so far as it lies within our power to do so.

The second method of classroom communication is the discussion period, which differs from the lecture in that it gives much greater opportunity for the student to participate. The students are expected to research and contribute to the class discussion. The teacher's role is one of discussion leader or moderator. There are a number of types of discussions and discussion groups.

The third method of communication between teacher and student is the seminar. It is usually composed of a smaller group of students and is more subject centered. Often one or more students read an essay or paper, and the rest of the time is devoted to a discussion of that subject area.

The fourth method of the teacher-student communication relationship is the tutorial, which is usually a one-to-one communication situation and, therefore, is more student-centered than the seminar. The teacher is concerned with the development of an individual student in a particular subject area, and is able to determine the strong or weak points of that student and give individual help in the areas most needed.

There are other avenues of learning, such as independent study and various types of reading projects and research. There are also many variations, modifications and combinations of the four main methods mentioned above. These four main methods of communication in the teaching and learning processes (and their modifications) have definite advantages and disadvantages, especially under specific conditions, and these will be discussed in a later chapter, as an effort will be made to point out the places of communication breakdown and in making positive suggestions how to avoid or eliminate these barriers to communication.

COMMUNICATION — A TWO-WAY ROAD

Communication in any situation is always a two-way road, never a one-way street. Classroom communication involves both teacher and student in teaching and learning. Learning on the part of the student, after all, is the real and only legitimate aim and purpose of education. Sometimes, however, the roles are reversed as the teacher observes and learns from the student. Often there can develop a mutual stimulation in such an exchange of ideas. Richard Morton in his article, "Learning as Communication," pointed out that there must be a relationship and understanding between two parties before learning takes place.

> Learning as communication points to the fact that teaching seeks to establish mental and social relationship between two parties who find mutual satisfaction and profit in the exchange. In the act additions to knowledge are produced. With a truly reciprocal exchange of values and stimulus learning flourishes. Teaching is as much to stimulate and enrich communication as to inform. . . .
>
> At the heart of communication and learning is the mutual desire to set up a steady and continuing rapprochement between two learners, one of whom has the added responsibility of being a teacher. Sometimes we need to be reminded that the process of learning involves and stimulates much more than the acquisition of knowledge. When learning takes place, there is a sense of relationship between the teaching source and the learner.[15]

Learning is not only stimulated by communication, but learning stimulates communication. "When what is learned is really understood, the learner inevitably wants to communicate about it to others. There is always a dynamic and creative element in the experience."[16] In fact, this is the way teachers evaluate student learning (and at the same time evaluate their own effectiveness in communicating), by asking the students to communicate through written examinations or by oral replies to questions asked in class. We simply assume that if the student cannot communicate the knowledge supposedly gained, then really he has not acquired the information or knowledge in the first case. We often hear people say, "I know what I am trying to say, but I just can't express it." Communication in writing and speaking is thinking outwardly, and if a person cannot express an idea in word symbols, it is most likely because he does not actually know that which cannot be expressed.

We have also often heard teachers say that the best way to learn something is to try to teach that information to someone else, and many a teacher, especially a beginning instructor, has struggled much harder at the preparation of daily lessons in an effort to be able to communicate clearly to his (generally unsuspecting) students that which he had been exposed to in undergraduate and graduate levels but is now forced to put together into some form of communicable utterances. Just as the teacher does not fully understand and possess a fact or a subject unless and until it can be communicated to the students, so the students, to whom the teacher imparts knowledge and shares with them thoughts and concepts, must be able to explain these to others. In doing so, they are deepening their understanding and enriching their own learning, and until given this opportunity, they cannot be certain whether or not they have really learned a thing.

If thinking is muddled, and one simply has not thought things through thoroughly, if there are hasty conclusions (arrived at by inductive leaps), or fragmentary and undigested bits of information churning about in the mind, clear communication cannot be forthcoming and, therefore, is bound to break down. Effective communication can take place only when the thinking process is complete and there is something which can be expressed adequately via verbal, vocal and nonverbal communication symbols and signs, as well as bodily action. The teacher cannot share with others that which he or she does not possess. All of the course work and research is of no avail, unless the teacher can bridge the gap between theory and meaningful expressions in relevant terms for the students' clear understanding and practical application. Neither can the students be expected to clearly communicate to others in oral and written examinations that which has been presented to them by the teacher in confused and abstract manner.

The key to successful teaching lies in the growth and improvement of classroom communication — the ability of the teacher to adequately communicate to the student and the student's ability and opportunity to respond and demonstrate some competence in reproducing what he has learned, not by rote, but by formulating in his own words the facts and concepts that now illuminate his mind. The level of this flow of communicable ideas becomes indicative of the level of learning that has taken place (assuming, of course, that the teacher has communicated something worthy of sharing with others in student interaction).

During the entire class period (and much of the day outside of the class) the teacher is communicating through the medium of the spoken word, either in speaking or listening. Since communication through the use of language is so intrinsically related to the entire teaching and learning processes, it should, therefore, become a matter of greatest concern for all teachers in every type of teaching situation.

Semester after semester and year after year, the teacher should find pleasure and a great amount of satisfaction in the repeated attempts to communicate the course material more effectively. With each such conscious and thoughtful attempt the teacher will discover that not only are the students learning more readily, but that the very act of communicating the subject material has sharpened his own perception and knowledge.

Frederick Heslet made the point that actually in a classroom situation it is impossible not to communicate:

> One primary assumption made regarding communication is that it is impossible not to communicate. The student in even the last row of a lecture class is communicating something back to the lecturer regarding the information that he is communicating. The student has two limits: he cannot "physically leave the field," and he cannot non-commmunicate.[17]

What are the students communicating through silent bodily reactions? They are communicating disbelief, rejection, boredom, apathy or interest and even (at least on rare occasions) intellectual excitement (This will be further explored in the chapter on feedback). From the moment the teacher translates information and concepts or thought into language symbols which are reinforced with nonverbal cues, until the student reacts through oral or physical responses (good or bad, favorable or unfavorable), communication takes place many times during each class period. In fact, we might say there is a steady flow of communication going back and forth between students and teacher throughout the entire class period.

This type of communication is vital to the total educational process, as Richard Morton has pointed out:

> Learning ought to involve a continuing process of free communication between individuals and groups. They should first have acquired adequate knowledge. . . .
>
> Nothing happens until somebody communicates with someone else. Vital to the total educational process is that element which appears to come forth as an additional value when two or more individuals communicate effectively with each other. And to the information each gets is

added something associated with the person, the attitudes, the objectives and the situation of each.[18]

There are many characteristics and competencies that are responsible for effective teaching, and one must recognize that the overall effectiveness results from the total characteristics of a good teacher. Much of the research which has been conducted in an effort to determine teaching effectiveness (such as the studies of Witty and Bousfield) support the conclusions that one of the greatest factors in the characteristics of a good versus a poor teacher is the difference in personal style in communicating what the teacher knows. The focal point then of all teaching and learning centers in communication, and the obvious conclusion has been aptly expressed as follows:

> Indeed, a teacher stands or falls largely on his ability to communicate through language. If he is able to make his students understand his knowledge, his insights, or his values, he succeeds; if he fails to do so he fails as a teacher. An individual need not be a scholar to be an outstanding teacher, but he must be a good communicator.[19]

This, of course, does not imply that a teacher does not need to avail himself or herself of all the graduate study that can be gotten, for our first assumption is that the teacher is indeed an expert in his or her field and the first communication breakdown to be considered in this book is the lack of education and training. Many other areas will be suggested where communication in the classroom can and often does break down. Removing these barriers between teachers and students will not guarantee that the ultimate aims and objectives of higher education will be reached, but as Mayer expressed it, "Breaking down the barriers does not in itself produce creativity. But creative teachers are those who remove barriers between themselves and their students and as a result release their own and their students' creativeness."[20]

This book is based upon the following six assumptions:

1. The communication of information and concepts is the foundation of all learning, and without this communication there can be no personal or social development.
2. Speech is the primary method by which we communicate (Speech in this context refers to much more than matters relating to voice and diction, but includes all the verbal and nonverbal forms of expression and many psychological and

rhetorical principles).

3. The effectiveness of the educational process and the accomplishment of the aims and purposes of higher education as outlined in this chapter correlate with the effectiveness of the communication process.

4. Conversely, to the extent and intensity of the interferences in any or all steps of the communication chain, learning diminishes or becomes totally blocked.

5. Teacher training for positions in higher education almost totally ignores courses in teaching methods and practical training so vital to the teaching profession.

6. Lack of training or inadequate training and practice in the communication arts have resulted in gross inefficiency in teaching. Knowledge of the subject material is essential, but coupled with that knowledge must be the ability to communicate or share that knowledge with others.

NOTES

1. Norvelle, Lee: Fundamental objectives of a teacher of speech in 1935. *Quarterly Journal of Speech, 21*:73, February, 1935.
2. The Hale Report of the University Grants Committee, Hale, Sir E., Chairman: *Report of the Committee on University Teaching Method*. London, HMSO, 1964. Paragraph 30.
3. Collier, K.G.: An experiment in university teaching, *Universities Quartely, 20*:336, June 1966.
4. Editorial: American Association of University Professors, May, 1933, quoted in *Improving College and University Teaching, 17*:175, 1969.
5. Rothwell, C. Easton, Chairman, Committee on Undergraduate Teaching: *The Importance of Teaching*. New Haven, Conn., The Hazen Foundation, 1968, p. 53.
6. Hough, John, and Durant, James: *Teaching: Description and Analysis*. Reading, Mass., Addison-Wesley, 1970, p. 21.
7. Hills, Philip: *Teaching and Learning as a Communication Process*. London, Croom Helm Ltd., 1979, pp. 13, 20.
8. Monroe, Alan: *Principles and Types of Speech*, 6th ed. Glenview, Illinois, Scott, Foresman and Co., 1967, pp. 28-31.
9. Berlo, David Kenneth: *Process of Communication; an Introduction to Theory and Practice*. New York, Holt, Reinhart and Winston, Inc., 1960, pp. 30-32.

10. Shannon, Claude, and Weaver, Warren: *The Mathematical Theory of Communication*. Urbana, University of Illinois Press, 1959 p. 4-6.
11. Peters, R.S. (Ed.): *John Dewey Reconsidered*. London, Routledge and Kegan Paul, 1977, p. 19.
12. Peters, R.S. (Ed.): *John Dewey Reconsidered*. p. 20.
13. Robbins Report: *Higher Education*. Appendix Two (B). London, HMSO, 1963, p. 582.
14. Rothwell: *The Importance of Teaching.*, p. 44.
15. Morton, Richard K.: Learning as communication. *Improving College and University Teaching, 19*:143, 144, 1971.
16. Morton: Learning as Communication, p. 144.
17. Heslet, Frederick E.: Communication pragmatics of the lecture, *Improving College and University Teaching, 19*:191, 1971.
18. Morton, Richard K.: Education as free communication. *Improving College and University Teaching, 19*:220, 1971.
19. Grambs, Jean Dresden, Carr, John C., and Fitch, Robert M.: *Modern Methods in Secondary Education*. 3rd ed. New York, Holt, Rinehart and Winston, Inc., 1958, p. 83.
20. Mayer, Frederick: Creative teaching. *Improving College and University Teaching, 8, No. 1*:42, Winter, 1960.

Part II
THE TEACHER
Educational and Social Backgrounds

CHAPTER 2

EDUCATION AND TRAINING FOR CLASSROOM LECTURES

An indispensable element in professional competence is mastery of one's own field. It scarcely need to be said that mastery means more when it is broad rather than parochial, when it is dynamic and creative rather than purely informational and static.

Rothwell

There have been numerous attempts to analyze "effective teaching" so that it can be handled objectively. Of all the factors listed in attempts at quantitative analysis, the outstanding one is the ability to communicate effectively.

Schwartz

ACCORDING to the communication model outlined in Chapter 1, the very first step in the complex communication chain must take place in the mind of the speaker. There must be some definite idea, concept or knowledge worthy of sharing with others. It is assumed, first of all, that the undergraduate and graduate preparation for college and university teaching will include in its curriculum a significantly large number of courses in the field of specialization, providing the prospective teacher with ample information and experience in the specific subject area in which he plans to teach.

It is superfluous to state that mastery of one's own particular field of learning is indispensable to professional competence. This training implies much more than merely the acquisition of factual information. It infers a breadth and depth of insight and involvement with the creative aspects of a specific subject area, as well as understanding of related and general areas of knowledge. For example, educational and general psychology can supply the prospective college and university teacher with theories of learning and motivation and assist in personality development, which will enable the teacher to enjoy a healthy relationship with the students.

A carefully planned curriculum may adequately prepare the future teacher with essential subject material necessary to begin a lifetime of teaching, but far less emphasis, and in many cases, no course work or practical training has been either required or made available, which will enable the teacher to communicate the learning and experience to those students who will be enlightened or bored for one or many semesters or academic terms under his tutelage.

Over a century ago, Daniel Gilman, first president of Johns Hopkins University, alluded to this problem, when in his inaugural address he urged the institutions responsible for training teachers to include a program which would develop teaching ability for the future professors.

In more recent years, Charles Süsskind, in his article, "On Teaching Science Teachers to Teach," expressed this same concern which has been largely unheeded throughout the decades. "More recently, the President's Commission on Higher Education has bewailed the fact that college teaching is the only major learned profession for which there does not exist a well-defined program of preparation directed toward developing the skills which it is essential for the practitioner to possess."[1]

He also referred to the report of the University of Chicago's Committee on Preparation of Teachers, in which the responses from 363 collegiate institutions were tabulated, indicating that "the large majority of the respondents believe that definite instruction in the art of teaching ought to be given as a part of the graduate program of the prospective college teacher."[2] The same acknowledgement of a woeful lack of training in the "how to teach" area of undergraduate and graduate program was revealed in the investigations carried out under grants from the Ford Foundation's Fund for the Advancement of Education.

A number of years ago, this problem was noted by T. H. Matthews, then Hon. Secretary of the National Conference of Canadian Universities. In an article, entitled "The Training of University Teachers," he wrote the following:

> In recent years there have been many discussions about the subjects which a university student should study and the integration of the separate themes of his work into a harmonious whole. . . . Unfortunately, far less attention has been directed towards the quality of university teaching itself and to the training of teachers in the techniques of their art. Yet surely the best of plans will fail if lecturers are not reasonably competent at their job. The question of ends — "What shall we teach?" must be followed by the question of means — "How shall we teach?"; and both must be effectively answered if we are to do our duty by our students. The well-balanced diet of the learned doctors may end in indigestion if the cooking is bad and the meals unattractively served.[3]

In the preparation of the manuscript for his book, *The Education of American Teachers*, James Conant visited twenty-seven institutions of higher education in twenty-two states, including such institutions as Harvard, Yale, Purdue, Indiana University, Ball State, Notre Dame, Vanderbilt, etc. He discovered a great amount of variety in the requirements for both education courses and practice teaching for elementary and secondary teaching. The minimum requirement of practice teaching was ninety clock hours, the maximum was three hundred. In an earlier study of the education course requirements in 294 institutions, he found a range for elementary teachers was eighteen to sixty-nine semester hours, and for secondary teachers ten to fifty-one. The first professional course, however, was not taken until the third year of college. Conant found that many of the education courses were "eclectic courses" as one entitled "Introduction to Teaching" at a well-known university. Concerning it, he wrote: "This course is even more of a potpourri, since bits of educational psychology and references to the literature on instructional methods have been stewed in. . . . The eclectic courses may be said to be a conglomeration of bits of history of American education, the philosophy of education, educational sociology, the economics and politics of the school, together with an introduction to education as a profession."[4]

State law requirements and teaching certification (compulsory) requisitions for completion of a certain number of education courses and hours or semesters of practice teaching ensure some degree of knowledge and training in communication skills. Even though some of these courses may be a conglomeration of information and the practice teaching may not be properly supervised, the student preparing for elementary and secondary school teaching has been exposed to theory and experience that should be of some definite benefit in the classroom. Concerning methods courses for these levels of teaching, Conant wrote:

> While all the instructions with which I am familiar required special methods courses for secondary teachers, by no means all required a general methods course. The more one is inclined to believe in a well-developed corpus of knowledge about how to teach (a science of education, if you will), the more one is ready to accept the idea of a general methods course. Yet in none of the twenty-seven institutions whose programs I analyzed in detail was more than one course (three semester hours) required.[5]

It has always seemed very strange that although education courses, methods courses and practice teaching have been required of the prospective elementary and secondary levels, actually none of these, generally speaking, are required of the future college and university professors. Before beginning my career as college teacher, I *chose* education as a minor area of study in my masters and doctoral studies, even though my major was in public address and communication skills. I could, however, have decided upon a completely unrelated minor as well as major areas of study and gotten a degree which would have made me "eligible" to teach on the college and university levels.

It is true that some of my classmates (comparatively few) did receive some practical training — somewhat unguided in teaching assistantships. Concerning assistantships, Conant made the following observation:

> I found other unfortunate practices in many colleges: the use of graduate students as teaching assistants placed in charge of "sections" of freshman courses; heavy dependence on anthologies and textbooks; pretentious reading lists, which only a few students take seriously; and lectures poorly delivered by uninspired teachers.[6]

The same general situation exists in Great Britain, with the exception that the future teacher has perhaps a better background and personal experience in communicating effectively. In the first place, public speaking and communication skills as such are not taught in higher education (nor in any other level for that matter, except in connection with the theatre or remedial speech and speech pathology). On the subject of "Talking to Large Groups," Arthur Wise wrote of reliance upon this personal background and experience to see one through in classroom communication:

> Let us accept that, as university teaching exists at the moment, a considerable amount of the teacher's time is spent in talking to large groups of students and in preparing for such talking. Whether in such a situation we can communicate successfully what we wish to communicate, depends almost entirely on our personal background and on what we may have gleaned from experience. It does not depend on the kind of Speech Education process that a lecturer has been through, because no such process exists for the university teacher.[7]

Surely he must be referring to the Speech and Drama education, or elocution, for which there is little use in practical university teaching. Because of the personal background and experience of some teachers in higher education in Great Britain, they are able to communicate to their students through the lecture method, even though they did not have any specific training for this particular task. Arthur Wise pointed out that anyone with a good home background could likewise be competent in lecturing. "There is no reason to suppose that the new university teacher will be any more competent in lecturing than would be the butcher, the baker or the candlestick maker."[8] But then how about those who do not have such a good personal background and experience to fall back upon when communicating what they have learned in teacher preparation or subject material?

Wise suggested an educational program that will assure communication skills in the classroom for every teacher, "We can only guarantee lecturing competence by some deliberate educational intervention, some process that sets out to develop the speech skill of a person who will spend much of his professional life trying to impart information and attitudes in oral terms."[9] In order to guarantee that every university teacher has competence in handling speech for communication purposes when lecturing to large groups of students, Wise recommended that "ideally, every university should be equipped to conduct such courses for its own staff."[10] He added, "but at the moment very few British universities have a Speech Educationist on the staff, and it would be more realistic to suggest intensive courses of the three-day crash type such as have been pioneered in industry."[11]

A survey carried out by the University of Leeds Department of Education indicated that "some 33% of graduate teachers in training were found to have speech that was in some way unsatisfactory for classroom communication purposes."[12]

I have discussed this matter of the "how to teach" courses with my teaching colleagues in America, and with a number of college professors in England, where, during a sabbatical, I wrote the manuscript for this book. In almost every instance the reply to my question, "what training did you receive in your undergraduate and graduate studies which specifically prepared you to organize and deliver a lecture or direct a discussion or seminar group?" the answer was the same, "absolutely none."

I had an interview with Roy Cox, one of the three senior lecturers of the University Teaching Method Unit of the University of London, (now called "The Centre for Staff Development in Higher Education"). His evaluation of the situation outlined above echoed the same lack of preparation in these areas for college and university teachers in Great Britain. The University Teaching Method Unit is desperately endeavoring in some way to remedy, at least partially, this deficiency in teacher training by conducting periodic three to five day workshops for teachers, a portion of which time is devoted to communication skills, methods and techniques in theory, and practical application. Other short and longer programs are also conducted by this group which include a large variety of related areas, such as staff development, assessment of studies, course design and student evaluation. The University of London Teaching Methods Unit is also responsible for publishing and reprinting books on teaching in higher education. The work of this organization and some of its publications will be mentioned later in this chapter.

The adage "those who can, do; those who can't, teach" suggests that not all the brains are to be found in the teaching profession, and that, perhaps, it takes less effort and intelligence to prepare and survive in the teaching profession than in many other professions which demand an initial and continued level of competency and excellence in a highly competitive business world or technological age (or to simply keep afloat in general society). It may well be that for many ambitious youths there exists a greater challenge in acquiring and maintaining a successful career outside the classroom than in qualifying for entrance into the teaching profession and remaining within the cloistered walls of an educational institution for the rest of their lives.

We live in a society and world of specialization. When we are in physical ill health we seek the services of a physician for diagnosis and treatment, and we feel confident that he has the ability to perform that for which he is being paid. We assume that he has received proper education in theory as well as ample, supervised practice during the period of internship, and keeps up with the latest developments and discoveries in the medical field. In time of legal requirements we accept advice and advocacy from our attorney, who, in order to remain in demand by clients, must have expert knowledge in matters of the law and must also keep abreast with the ever-changing regulations and legislation. We trust the educational training and skills acquired by the pilots of a jumbo jet, and feel confident that these are commensurate to the task of navigating the plane (and us) safely to a predetermined destination. And so the list could go on through the various professions.

This same expertise is expected of a college and university teacher who has a background of five to seven or eight years of pre-professional and professional training. Students who pay high costs of tuition today have every right to expect teachers to know the area of their specialization and to communicate that knowledge effectively. Students are often willing to tolerate other failings in the teaching profession, but are quick and harsh in evaluating their instructors as to whether they know what they are talking about, and also whether they know how to convey their knowledge and experience on to them.

If the teacher as communicator does not have clear ideas and concepts in his own mind because of a lack of acquiring the needed knowledge, then the very first step in the communication process has been blocked, resulting in an obvious major communication breakdown in teaching. Thinking is really talking to oneself, and speaking is thinking out loud, and so we can say that the first step in communication begins within the mind of the teacher as he clearly "talks" to himself. The instructor can obviously not communicate to his students ideas or the meaning of experience unless these have initially been stored in the mind. The teacher must receive, then understand and incorporate these ideas and experiences into his life, and these must arouse personal reactions and feelings. The teacher must first discover "truth" before any attempt is made to help the students discover it for themselves. In summary then, we might say that the initial education, background and training (plus a lifetime of continued study and experience) must fulfill the many prerequisites of communication — two of which are the following: having something worthy to say, and being to convey these thoughts effectively to others.

K. Patricia Cross, Visiting University Professor, Office of Vice President for Academic Affairs at the University of Nebraska, and past president of the American Association for Higher Education, presented a paper, "The Instructional Revolution" at Concurrent General Session in Chicago. In this presentation she enumerated the reasons an instructional revolution is necessitated in the American ideal of college education for all. She pointed out that years of experience or even scholarly reputation are not necessarily related to the quality of undergraduate instruction, and expressed the hope that this common practice of pretending that experience and scholarship guarantee good college teaching should not be perpetuated.

In a caricaturing paraphrase, Patricia Cross reduced to absurdity the respected scholar who knows a lot about his discipline but very little, if anything, about the learning theories and process of teaching methods and techniques. After listening to a scholar addressing a workshop on instructional improvement, she applied this same spirit and "logic" to an address which the same scholar might present at a meeting of scientists concerning their area of speciality.

> I have never had a course on teaching, and I know nothing of the various theories of learning. (This confession is usually made with pride rather than humility.) I have, however, taught in a college classroom for twenty-five years. While I am not familiar with so-called teaching methods and techniques, I hope that my experience and observations will be helpful and useful to other teachers.
>
> There is, of course, no real science of education in the sense that experts can predict with certainty who will succeed in college, nor do we

know how to create the most desirable learning conditions. Therefore, it seems to me that I, who am in the classroom every day can probably be as helpful in understanding learning as can researchers who rarely teach in the reality of the classroom.

While I admit that there are some techniques that can probably be used to improve the performance of the *average* teacher — instructional objectives and faculty evaluation perhaps — the master teacher is not dependent on tools and techniques. He has a sensitivity for learning — a feel for when real learning is taking place. A teacher who loves his subject and who personally experiences the joy of learning is probably in the best position to create such satisfaction for others.

This real life story is then paralleled to the following fantasy in which the professor with his years of personal experience with weather conditions will contribute important insight to a group of meteorologists at one of the workshops.

I have never studied meteorology, and I know nothing of the various theories on the subject. (This confession is usually made with humility rather than pride.) I have, however, lived in the physical world for forty-five years. While I have no idea what causes certain weather patterns or how to induce rain when we need it, I do put on the snow tires in winter and carry an umbrella when it rains. I hope my experience and observations will be helpful and useful to professional meteorologists.

There is, of course, no real science of weather in the sense that experts can predict with certainty whether it will rain on a given day, nor do we know how to bring about the most desirable weather conditions. Therefore, it seems to me that I, who live with the weather every day, can probably be as helpful in understanding it as can researchers who rarely venture into the reality of a rainstorm or a blizzard.

While I admit that there are some techniques that can probably be used to improve the performance of the average meteorologist — barometers and weather maps perhaps — the master meteorologist is not dependent on tools and techniques; he has a sensitivity to the weather, and perhaps a good arthritic knee. A meteorologist who loves weather and who personally experiences the joys of beautiful days is probably in the best position to create such satisfaction for others.[13]

I would now like to bring back this professor from this ludicrous and incongruous scene of unrealisitic "make-believe" to another real life situation, and I wish to point out another paradoxical parallel in which this scholar (or any other academician) with his years of experience might address a group of educators at a workshop on teaching methods, techniques and communication skills.

I have actually never had any formal training in public speaking and know nothing about teaching methods nor communication theories. (This confession is usually made with pride, rather than humility.) I have, however, been living in a gregarious society for forty-five years. While I have never paid any particular attention to such things as voice and diction or the use of rhetorical devices and style, or worried myself concerning precise organization of my teaching material, I hope that my experience and observations will compensate for my lack of formal training along these lines.

There is, of course, no real science of methods of presentation, since one cannot predict with certainty that these will result in every case with successful teaching. It is more important that I have the knowledge of the subject than a particular technique or various elocutionary powers. It, therefore, seems to me that I, who have used speech all of my life, need to pass on my knowledge in simple words as ideas and concepts come to my mind. Truth is not dependent upon any certain mode of expression, and, anyway, it is the students' responsibility to capture these words of wisdom as they are transferred to them.

While I admit that there are some techniques that could probably be used to improve the performance of the average lecturer (training in public speaking, voice and diction, oral interpretation, discussion techniques, logic, theories of motivation and principles of persuasion) the master lecturer is not dependent on tools and techniques. A teacher who knows and loves his subject and who personally experiences the joys of talking to his students need not be unduly concerned as to whether he adequately communicates his own knowledge to others or inspires them to search for the solution to life's problems.

TEACHERS HIRED ON BASIS OF SCHOLARSHIP

The most important qualities considered in hiring a college or university teacher or in determining basic pay scale, annual salary raises or ranking are the degrees earned in a specific area and the teaching experience acquired, as though these can be more or less automatically equated with knowledge and teaching abilities or qualifications in the use of methods, techniques and the application of psychological and rhetorical concepts of learning and communication. There is, however, no attempt being made to depreciate and underestimate the importance of scholarship. As mentioned earlier in this chapter, it is obvious and virtually taken for granted that a college or university teacher be an expert in a specific subject area, and there can be no real communication unless there first is knowledge.

In the preface of the book *Improving Teaching in Higher Education*, compiled by David Jackson and David Jaques, it was observed that scholarship and research are acknowledged as primariy qualities for hiring teachers, but the task of transmitting the end product of this scholarship and research has been relegated to a secondary concern and left largely to the student to get what he can of what is being handed out to him.

> New teachers in higher education tend to be appointed because of their demonstrated or potential achievement in the pursuit of excellence in scholarship and research. These traditionally valued characteristics are still highly prized particularly within the university culture, and the maintenance of high standards of scholarship and the pursuit of original research continued to hold a pre-eminent and overriding importance in the eyes of both individual academics, and university promotion boards. It has been taken for granted that when it comes to the "secondary" task of transmitting this scholarship and research to the next generation, the role of the lecturer is that of "expert" and "authority" and that the major responsibility for the learning process, the process of acquiring the expert knowledge lies with the student.[14]

One reason given for this "secondary" place alloted to teaching performance is that it takes an increasing amount of effort and time simply to keep up with the increased knowledge in an area of specialization in addition to pressures often exerted upon the teacher to engage in further research. The teacher may have little time to do more than hand out chunks of information without regard for an equitable method of presentation of this knowledge.

The conclusion reached in the previously mentioned preface, points out the obvious fact that anyone who will dedicate his whole life to teaching ought to be concerned not only with scholarship, but equally be prepared for the task of communicating this scholarship. Teachers are to "dedicate themselves not to a few months of anxious concern, but to a lifetime of involvement in the matching of excellence in scholarship with the skilled teaching performance,"[15] even though this is to ask for "a considerable sacrifice of time and effort which is unrecognized and unrewarded."[16] We can observe the irony in the fact that academicians and scholars with such a great store of "analytical powers of the mind, so rarely apply those powers when considering their own teaching, whatever the reasons for the reluctance may be."[17]

Peter Banks cited an illustration in which "the students in one college of education found it ironic that a lecturer in education and teaching method should himself be incapable of communicating effectively."[18]

Since there are few teaching technique courses offered either on the undergraduate or graduate level and speech training is virtually nonexistent throughout Great Britain, and since, in many American colleges and universities, education in teaching methods of training in the art of public speaking and in oral communications are on an "elective" basis (with some possible exception of a single two- to three-semester hour fundamental speech course), it is not very difficult to see why the teacher in higher education, with all of the years of training, and, perhaps, several degrees behind his name, goes out of the "training" program almost totally unprepared to communicate to the students the expertise thus far acquired.

In 1973, Margaret King carried out a survey of university lecturers, either still in training or newly entering the profession, and she wrote the replies in her article entitled "The Anxieties of University Teachers." The respondents expressed anxiety in such things as stage fright when facing a large (or small) class of students, or general lack of confidence in themselves and in their role of teacher personality. They had fears concerning the selection and sufficiency of material to present to their students, and actually in not knowing how to prepare and organize their lectures. They confessed having poor speaking ability in several or all of the following areas — content and form, from preparation to delivery, including organization and synthesis of information, with rate, projection, voice quality, the proper use of nonverbal as well as the verbal aspects of communication, and maintaining attention and interest or providing proper motivation for learning. Some respondents expressed great concern with the understanding of their relationship with, and feedback and reactions from their students.[19]

Many of these anxieties and feelings of personal inadequacy, lack of self-confidence, and nervousness are quite normal patterns of behavior for anyone who performs in public. In most cases one can learn to control these attitudes and feelings, but without proper education and training it is easy to see why so many lecturers resort to reading their scripts, but here again, they probably have never received any previous training in script writing or in the art of oral interpretation or reading out loud, and, therefore, they are no better prepared to read their script than to deliver their lectures extemporaneously!

Ellis and Jones in their article "Anxiety about Lecturing" agreed with Margaret King that giving lectures causes new university teachers more anxiety than any other form of teaching, and listed the various forms that such anxiety takes, also observing the means employed in dealing with these situations by normal (not neurotic) people. Among the diverse means often used in erroneous attempts at coping with these inadequacies that the individual teacher perceives, Ellis and Jones included such actions as using jargon, keeping to a prepared script, even distortion to hide the lecturer's ignorance, dogmatism, a submissive or overcritical approach, a too theoretical approach, excessive reliance on empirical evidence or histrionics or acting (faking).[20]

HOW TO PROVIDE ADEQUATE TEACHER TRAINING FOR CLASSROOM LECTURING

Formal Courses

Since there admittedly exists in many cases a total lack or, at least, an inadequate minimum of teaching method courses and training in communication skills in the educational background of the average college and university teacher, a much greater concern should be shown toward strengthening these areas of weakness, and a much greater emphasis must be given in the development of the curriculum to include some of the following courses (and noncurricular activities).

Somewhere in the undergraduate educational study program, several courses dealing directly with the training in communicative skills should be required of every individual who plans to enter college and university teaching. Whenever possible, a minor in speech education would provide an excellent background preparation for those who, for the entire period of professional life will stand daily before inquiring, critical or apathetic audiences.

At least one advanced course in communication should be included in the graduate program of the prospective college and university teacher, as well as a genuine teaching methods course.

Practice Teaching

Provisions should be made in the undergraduate and graduate programs for the supervision of practice teaching. This should be administered by experienced professors, who are themselves competent in background training and actual experience in the areas of teaching methods and communication. This supervision should include repeated student presentation of "typical" classroom lectures, either in one of the previously mentioned classes followed by classroom (oral and written) evaluation by a qualified professor and fellow students.

Assistantships

Far greater potential could be utilized in the graduate assistantship, fellowship or internship plans. Here are excellent opportunities for not only financial aid but practice and development in these vital areas of practical training, the outcome of which can make the difference between a successful or mediocre professional career. Comparatively few future college teachers elect or are given the opportunity to participate in such a program.

There are a few universities which have developed such programs in conjunction with the doctorate degree. In the book *Improving College Teaching*, Wise outlined one of these plans:

> In most cases the Ph.D. candidate engages in part-time teaching over a period of two years. During his first year of teaching responsibility he works under the close supervision of a senior faculty member but has opportunity to lecture and to lead class discussions with help and supervision from his senior colleague. . . . In the best of these programs several members of the departmental faculties work closely with the teaching assistants.[21]

Harvard University offers an internship program which consists of a five-year doctorate schedule with financial assistance. During the first three years the candidates study toward the doctoral degree, the following year is spent in teaching, and the final year is used to complete the dissertation.[22]

At the Washington University in St. Louis, the History Department operates a similar four-year program leading to the doctorate. This is one of the five universities which have received grants from the Danforth Foundation to aid the inexperienced teacher to develop teaching skills. This plan can be summarized in the following three steps:

> 1. Toward the close of the first year of graduate study students visit discussion sections of history courses taught by members of the department. These brief visits are followed by discussion of problems in teaching that have been raised by the students. In the summer following the first year of study, the students prepare for teaching assignments by spending their full time in reading. Toward the close of the summer they meet with members of the history faculty in a two-day conference on teaching and graduate preparation.

> 2. During their second and third years the graduate students teach under supervision in two history courses. In addition to accepting considerable responsibility for the discussion sections of these courses, the graduate students lecture two to four times a year. In one course, they also supervise honors theses and, in addition, assist in preparing the examinations.

> 3. All members of the History Department faculty participate in supervising the work of the teaching assistants.[23]

In a few of the graduate institutions such as Yale, grant funds have been used to finance internships to enable the student or beginning Ph.D. graduate to obtain practical teaching experience. During this internship period, members of the teaching faculty provide some supervision. Students who are working on their dissertations or have already received their Ph.D. at Antioch College are offered a type of internship in which they teach half time, under supervision of experienced faculty members. In some institutions of higher education graduate students receive financial assistance while teaching under supervision in neighboring colleges.[24]

Summer Schools for Lecturers

The preceding four areas of theory and practice have been suggested as solutions to the problem of communication breakdown in teaching, resulting from a lack of education and training, related to courses and programs from the undergraduate and graduate student (and recent graduate) *prior* to entering as a full-time instructor in the teaching career. There are many students, however, to whom these programs are not available (or who did not avail themselves of these courses and programs during their student days).

In 1947, a paper was presented to the National Conference of Canadian Universities, the thesis of which was to advocate a short summer school for university teachers where they could obtain practical training in teaching methods and lecturing. In June, 1950, the first three weeks' course was held at the Royal Military College at Kingston, Ontario. The Canadian universities were expected to pay most of the expenses, but some universities did not send any of their teachers to this experimental session.

The idea and general plan were excellent, especially in view of the fact that these "students" from all parts of Canada ranged from junior lecturers to full professors, who, obviously, sensed their lack of proper training before entering the teaching profession and were now anxious to avail themselves of such a three-week summer session of practical work. Each morning a student was required to present a fifteen minute introductory lecture of a course he taught. This introductory lecture included the general plan and outline of the course, discussion of the textbook and additional reading requirements, an explanation of the purpose and method of the course, as well as the relation of the subject matter to other fields of study. Each lecture was recorded and later played back to the student in the presence of an instructor or fellow "student." After each presentation, members of the audience offered criticism or evaluated the organization and delivery of the lecture. A general discussion followed. One of the staff who was an authority in speech presented an initial lecture on how to lecture and provided an evaluation sheet for each one in the audience to fill out while listening to these student speeches.

T.H. Matthews, in describing the evaluation which took place, enumerated the various areas of critical judgment:

> The main question was, of course, "Did the speech achieve its object?"; but in addition comments were invited upon the important de-

tails which might contribute to the success or failure of the performance. Had the speaker any monotonous or annoying gestures? Did he look at his audience or address someone outside a side window? Could every word be heard? Did he establish a friendly relation with his listeners? Was his argument clear and well presented? Did he use jargon? Was there too much or too little material for the time? And so on. These simple forms greatly aided the students in making their observations, and the level of criticism as well as the level of speaking rose as the course proceeded. The comments were frank but friendly and were often reopened at voluntary evening sessions when performers and critics would gather round a tape machine to replay and re-analyse the speech.[25]

The tape recorders were used not only to listen to the tapes after the speeches were presented, but by each speaker in preparation of the lecturer before delivering it. Each student presented at least three speeches, and some students during a special session, read papers, just as though these were to be presented to a university conference.

During this summer session theory was combined with practice. There were a number of other staff lectures on such subjects as "What are the general qualities of a good speech?" "Preparing notes for a lecture," "The student's notes, " etc. The lectures of the summer session staff were likewise discussed and evaluated. These instructors who attended this summer session as students, felt that this brief course helped to fill a need which has not been met in the regular undergraduate and graduate training. One student wrote, "Having had very little previous experience in lecturing, I feel that I received enormous benefit from my three weeks at Kingston. The course had great practical value in that it dealt with so many of the problems which bother an instructor new at teaching. . . . Personally, I shall attack my assignment for next year with new confidence and with an interest and enthusiasm which I did not have before."[26]

In laying plans for this summer session the following comparison was made: "Other platform artists such as concert violinists take many lessons and spend laborious hours in practice before they give a public performance. University lecturers normally do neither, and the school was suggested as a means of providing an opportunity for both."[27]

It is obvious that such a brief concentrated course cannot undo all of the poor speech habits of a lifetime acquired thus far, nor be a substitute for three or more semesters of speech training.

Workshops

Three- to five-day workshops have been conducted between semesters or terms or just prior to the opening of the regular term,
such as the one already mentioned which is sponsored by the University Teaching Method Unit of the University of London. These
workshops bring together teachers from a wide variety of disciplines
to discuss common problems such as evaluation of teaching, student
assessment, and the design and evaluation of courses. This "Course
for Lecturers" as it is titled, is offered for the purpose of developing
skills in methods of teaching, such as lecturing, running seminars
and tutorials. These workshops are generally attended by over a
hundred teachers, who, for one thing, come prepared to write out
and deliver a ten to fifteen minute classroom lecture, which is discussed and evaluated by the group in a seminar setting. These lectures are video-taped for later viewing, listening and evaluation.

Special Courses Available During Academic Year

From the short workshops, conducted by the University Teaching Unit of the University of London during the past few years a
one- to two-year course has evolved, at the end of which a diploma
in Teaching and Course Development is awarded. This course can
be taken by those already engaged in teaching, and can be taken on
a full-time (one year) or part-time (two years) basis. One day a week
the participants meet from 2 PM to 9 PM. There are two practical sessions of one and one-half hours consisting of exercises or collabora-
tive course work. The two theory sessions of one and one-half hours
in length may take the form of a seminar or private study. The participants are expected to attend three or four workshops during the
course. During the year they are also required to complete the four
following items: (1) A practical, consisting of showing a degree of
competence in various modes of teaching; (2) A report that involves
the design or evaluation of a course from the participant's own department; (3) A project based on the participant's own department;
and (4) An essay of 4,000 to 8,000 words.

Commenting on the dual emphasis of the University Teaching Method Unit on course design and communication skills, Chris Furedy, of York University, agreed that "attaining competence as a public speaker is a legitimate concern and no one would deny that mastery of good communication skills is central to the effective use of the lecture method." He, however, questioned whether we should not place a greater emphasis on course design and modes of student learning, which includes studying the need of the students, course construction, student selection, teaching methods and assessment of teaching.[28]

Faculty Evaluation and Student Evaluation

Whether the teacher has had courses in teaching methods and public speaking or not, a continuing program of faculty evaluation by students, fellow faculty or administrators will be most helpful and worthwhile if carried out in a constructive, systematic manner.

Personal Endeavors to Improve Teaching Performance

On a voluntary basis, from time to time, a teacher can exchange evaluations and observations with his or her colleagues in or out of the department. Several instructors can observe each other and make helpful suggestions. Occasionally, a lecture can be tape-recorded or even videotaped and evaluated either individually or with a colleague.

The problem with many of the workshop and summer session evaluations is that the situations under which the lectures are presented are artificial, since either there is no real student or classroom environment or the one to be evaluated has devoted disproportionately more time and effort into a brief "typical" lecture. This is also true of the annual or semiannual teaching evaluation by faculty or administrators, because such an evaluation of a specific class lecture has been prearranged and particularly well prepared by the lecturer (probably on a favorite topic). How about the other 100 lectures and discussions during the year given by the average teacher to which the students are subjected several times a week; how do they compare with the specific ones designed and designated for critical analysis?

In rating a good teacher, students often place knowledge of the subject material and communication skills at the top of the list in importance. Unless the teacher is knowledgeable in his discipline and is able to transfer this knowledge to the students — in other words, unless there is something to teach them and the ability to communicate it effectively, the learning process deteriorates or becomes totally blocked. The *Report of Commission on Teaching in Higher Education* presented to Liverpool Conference, April, 1969, stated:

> A new lecturer has a great deal to learn. He has to adjust himself either to a completely new environment or else to being on the other side of what is still very much a fence, to progress in one step from being taught to teaching itself. The arts and techniques of lecturing are complex. To assume that a lecturer entering the profession will automatically have satisfactory abilities in this direction is, of course, nonsense. Those who teach in schools have to be trained for the task and it is irrational to consider similar training unnecessary for teachers in higher education. Lecturing is a science, not an acquired taste; as such it can be transmitted, learnt and improved upon.[29]

NOTES

1. Süsskind, Charles: On teaching science teachers to teach, *Improving College and University Teaching*, 5, *No. 1*:46, 1957.
2. Süsskind, Charles: On teaching science teachers to teach, pp. 46, 47.
3. Matthews, T.H.: The training of university teachers, *Universities Quarterly*, 5, *No. 3*:269, May, 1951.
4. Conant, James Bryant: *The Education of American Teachers*. New York, McGraw-Hill Book Co., Inc., 1963, pp. 128, 129.
5. Conant, James Bryant: *The Education of American Teachers*. p. 138.
6. Conant, James Bryant: *The Education of American Teachers*. p. 78.
7. Wise, Arthur: Talking to large groups. In Layton, David (Ed.): *University Teaching in Transition*. Edinburgh, Oliver and Boyd, 1968, p. 35.
8. Wise, Arthur: Talking to large groups. p. 35.
9. Wise, Arthur: Talking to large groups. pp. 35, 36.
10. Wise, Arthur: Talking to large groups. p. 40.
11. Wise, Arthur: Talking to large groups. p. 40, 41.
12. Wise, Arthur: Talking to large groups. p. 40.
13. Cross, K. Patricia: *The Instructional Revolution*, (mimeographed). Paper presented at Concurrent General Session, I 31st National Conference on

Higher Education, sponsored by American Association for Higher Education. Chicago, Monday, March 8, 1976, pp. 4, 5.

14. Jackson, David, and Jaques, David (Eds.): *Improving Teaching in Higher Education.* London, University Teaching Methods Unit, 1976, Preface, p. 5.

15. Jackson, David, and Jaques, David (Eds.): *Improving Teaching in Higher Education.* p. 6.

16. Jackson, David, and Jaques, David (Eds.): *Improving Teaching in Higher Education.* p. 6.

17. Jackson, David, and Jaques, David (Eds.): *Improving Teaching in Higher Education.* p. 6.

18. Banks, Peter E.: Lecturing and all that, *Cambridge Journal of Education, 2, No. 1*:7, Lent, 1972.

19. King, Margaret: The anxieties of university teachers. *Universities Quarterly, 28*:69-83, Winter, 1973.

20. Ellis, H. P., and Jones, A. D.: Anxiety about lecturing, *Universities Quarterly, 29*:91-95, Winter, 1974.

21. Wise, Max: Who teaches the teachers? In Lee, Calvin B. T. (Ed.): *Improving College Teaching.* Washington, American Council on Education, 1967, pp. 82, 83.

22. Rothwell, C. Easton, Chairman, Report of the Committee on Undergraduate Teaching: *The Importance of Teaching.* New Haven, Conn., The Hazen Foundation, 1968, p. 70.

23. Wise: Who teaches the teachers? p. 84.

24. Wise: Who teaches the teachers? p. 83.

25. Matthews, T.H.: The training of university teachers. p. 271.

26. Matthews, T.H.: The training of university teachers. p. 274.

27. Matthews, T.H.: The training of university teachers. p. 269.

28. Furedy, Chris: Improving lecturing in higher education. *The Canadian Journal of Higher Education, 9, No. 1*:46, 47, 1979.

29. *Report of Commission on Teaching in Higher Education,* Presented to Liverpool Conference, April, 1969. London, National Union of Students, p. 48, Paragraphs 6, 7.

CHAPTER 3

IMPORTANCE OF PERSONALITY
IN THE CLASSROOM

If the teacher is to stimulate undergraduates and to draw them with some measure of enthusiasm into a partnership of intellectual or creative growth and discovery, he should, of course, have personal characteristics favorable to this outcome.

Rothwell

Teaching is a product of the total personality of the teacher.

Richard Morton

EVEN though a teacher may possess advanced academic qualifications and ample teaching experience as well as an adequate background in teaching methods and communicative skills, this does not guarantee effective classroom communication. We have seen in Chapter 1 that the communicative process involves the entire being and is greatly affected by the personality of the communicator. Student ratings of teaching effectiveness often place acceptable personality on an equal level with knowledge of subject and communicative skill. It would probably be safe to conclude that more learning can take place in the case of a "poor" teacher with a good personality than from an otherwise good teacher with a poor or unacceptable personality, who, consequently, has little or no rapport with the students.

PERSONALITY IN TEACHING

Aristotle considered ethical persuasion — the integrity and disposition of the speaker — as one of the three modes of persuasion and believed it to be as important or more influential than emotional and logical appeals. Cato, who lived over two millenniums ago, is credited with enunciating the important principle of associating personality as an intricate part of rhetoric. When defining oratory, he declared it to be "a good man speaking well." Ralph Waldo Emerson long ago observed that "who you are speaks so loudly I cannot hear what you say to the contrary."

The age-old question has been asked many times, "Which is more important, *what* a person says or *how* he says it?" — (Content versus form, to be discussed in a later chapter). These two important aspects of communication are not mutually exclusive. Similarly, one could question, "Which is more effective — *what* is said or by *whom* it is spoken?" Getzels and Jackson believe that

> The personality of the teacher is a significant variable in the classroom. Indeed some would argue it is the most signficant variable. The educational impact of an Ichabod Crane or a Mark Hopkins, of a Mr. Chips or a Socrates, is surely not due solely to what he knows, or even to what he does, but in a very real sense to what he is.[1]

Knowledge of the subject material and skills enabling one to effectively communicate this knowledge to others, obviously form a basis for classroom communication. What is actually heard and accepted by the hearers, however, may not depend so much on *what* is being said, nor even *how* it is spoken, but by *whom* it is said — on the nature of the personal relationship between the one instructing and the one learning. Personality plays such an intricate and important part in communication in teaching that it cannot be minimized or ignored. It can be one of the greatest factors in determining a teacher's success or failure, because learning involves a relationship between the teaching source and the learner. One who teaches effectively teaches not only his subject but himself. Personality is that part of the teacher's self which he projects into every classroom activity, thereby effecting and conditioning every learning situation.

Students scrutinize their instructors constantly, and this affects communication in the classroom for either good or bad, as brought out by Richard Rees:

> College teachers are viewed by students in a variety of ways. The personality, attitudes, teaching methods, and classroom effectiveness of each teacher are under constant scrutiny, and it seems reasonable that certain teacher characteristics are more favorable than others in contributing to meaningful classroom learning experiences.[2]

During registration, when making out a tentative or actual schedule of classes for the coming term, especially when there are a number of sections of the same subject from which to choose, often the deciding factor in the final selection by the student will be the answer to the question, "*Who* is teaching that section of the course?" Consciously or unwittingly, we associate a product or an idea with the person or persons representing or advocating it. The individual must, therefore, sell himself or herself before the product or proposition can be sold. This is a principle that is recognized and accepted in the business world. In radio and television, advertisers have learned to use the "star" of the show, who has already been accepted by that particular audience, to promote their product. This is sometimes referred to as the "halo effect," and advertisers at times take advantage of it and exploit the members of the public. They reason that if the viewers, listeners, or readers admire or "worship" their hero, they will be less apt to raise their defenses or resist the suggestions being advocated by the hero.

Likewise in the "business" of teaching, the teacher must sell himself before or during the time allotted for the presentation of the subject material. That is what communication is all about according to our original definition — sharing something with others — not only knowledge but one's self. It is only natural (and in agreement with the "laws" of psychology which govern our behavior to a large extent), that we will learn more from someone we like than from someone about whom we either do not know anything, or whom we dislike. Richard Morton elaborated on this point in his article, "Personal Backgrounds of Effective Teaching."

> Teaching is a product of the total personality of the teacher. . . .

Teaching will not be effective unless the instructor has a chance to put his personality over and really get to know his students. We learn from people, and we learn best when we like and respect the people and are in the midst of a happy situation. The class will learn much from an instructor's general character and philosophy and his experiences on a variety of themes, no matter what subject he teaches.[3]

Morton also voiced his opinion that institutions of higher education are just as much in need of teachers qualified in character, with a satisfactory philosophy of life and capacity for constructive adjustments, as teachers qualified by graduate study and classroom experience. He observed that teachers "sometimes teach poorly because their living techniques are no better than their teaching techniques. They have perhaps muddled their thinking and social relationships more than their lecture notes. Their view of their students and their subject matter is disturbed and distorted because a good deal more than that is distorted for them."[4]

Charles Glicksberg, in his article "What Makes a Classroom," stressed the importance of the teacher's personality and cited a number of ways in which communication in the learning process breaks down in the classroom when undesirable traits of personality are manifest by the one who is to instruct the students. The students must not be frightened or intimidated, so they will dread coming to class. It is up to the instructor to put them at ease. "They learn little from an instructor who resorts to the weapon of ridicule or sarcasm; they are afraid to speak out lest they make a mistake. The teacher is responsible for generating a constructive class spirit. During the very first session he must make the students feel that they will want to work cooperatively with him. . . . If he is wise, he will not bring his moods of boredom or depression into the classroom. His personal life should not be allowed to affect his teaching performance." Glicksberg then quoted a student's viewpoint concerning the disposition and personality of the instructor:

A good teacher is not simply one who knows a particular subject well. A good teacher is not simply one who lectures to a classroom. A good teacher is one who has an enthusiasm, not only for his subject but for life itself. He conveys this enthusiasm and vitality to his students in every word he speaks. He should give his all to his students so that he may expect all from them in return. He is not merely a figure in front of the classroom; he should be a spiritual force that constantly rekindles the human spirit. His character and moral strength should call forth faith and inspiration in every student. He should be a source of inspiration in communicating new ideas and in examining the values of the old.[5]

TEACHER PERSONALITY EXPERIMENTS

Experimental research backs up what has been already concluded by common sense and simple observation relative to the teacher's personality. In one experiment a test group of 231 second- and third-year college students were selected. Professors from the behavioral sciences presented lectures to these students whom they had never before met. Following the lectures, tests were given covering the material presented. A few days later another set of lecturers presented lectures in a similar manner to the same group of students. These professors were, however, acquainted with the students through counseling, social contacts, classes, discussions, etc. Following these lectures the students were again tested on the contents of the material presented with the results that the grades were 21 percent higher for the material covered by instructors they knew.[6]

Getzels and Jackson were able to locate 1,000 studies before 1950 and 800 since then relating to some aspect of the teacher's personality (from all levels of teaching). They cited The Teacher Characteristics Study directed by Ryans (1960) as the single most extensive study of teachers done to that date. This study identified and analyzed patterns of classroom behavior, attitudes, viewpoints, and intellectual and emotional qualities that may characterize teachers. During six years, about 100 separate research projects were carried out and more than 6,000 teachers in 1,700 schools and about 450 school systems participated. There were numerous separate findings that emerged from this extensive study, many of which are somewhat unrelated to the point under discussion here. General patterns of behavior characteristics were grouped together. (These will be mentioned later in the chapter.) An attempt was made to correlate the teachers characteristics with classroom behavior. In other words, the researchers endeavored to predict the teachers' classroom behavior following an assessment of their "symptoms" or personality traits.

"Much of the Teacher Characteristics Study was devoted to determining these *correlates* of teacher classroom behavior. Materials were selected and assembled into an instrument known as the Teacher Characteristic Schedule, an omnibus self-report inventory, made up of 300 multiple-choice and check-list items."[7]

At this point I would like to cite an interesting experiment to which I will allude again in a later chapter. A few years ago, the services of Michael Fox, a professional actor with years of experience in motion pictures, television and the theater were secured to deliver different types of lectures, varying in the portrayal of personality traits. "Dr. Fox," as he was referred to, was instructed to imitate two hypothetical professors who differed greatly in characteristics of expressiveness, such as might be associated with enthusiasm, humor, friendliness, charisma, and "personality." Given these narrative descriptions, the actor, because of his prior training and experience, was able to assume an appropriate role for each part on demand.[8]

Two groups of students with similar backgrounds heard and evaluated Michael Fox's lectures. One group heard him present a medium-content script delivered in a low-expressive manner, and the other group listened to the high-expressive delivery of the medium-content script. Each group was requested to evaluate the lecture in such areas as enthusiasm and dynamism. The student ratings of the lecture high in expressiveness were better than those of low-expressive lectures. These two groups of students were also given tests covering the content of the lecture, and, as might be expected, those who heard the high-expressive lecture achieved higher results. These findings correlate with the results of Coats and Smidchens study of audience recall as a function of speaker dynamism, in which it was concluded that audiences remember more from a dynamic lecture than from a static lecture.[9]

Reputation, as well as disposition and personality of the learning source, influences student achievement. This fact has been illustrated and demonstrated in a number of experiments in which various control groups of university students have listened to the same taped lecture, but each group was told that the speaker was a different person in a contrasting social or political position or role. The amount of change of opinion for or against the concept being advocated by the speaker was carefully measured for short-term and long-term effect. This reaction and change of opinion was largely influenced by the listener's perception of the personality and "ethos" of the speaker.

DEFINITION AND MEANING OF PERSONALITY

Personality can mean the way you look at yourself. It can mean how other people look at you or how you look at other people. We often hear the expression, "What a fine personality he has." This might mean that the person possesses those qualities that attracted the originator of the above statement. Personality can, in fact, mean almost anything to anyone. The word "personality" comes from the Latin *persona,* which referred to the mask worn by actors who played the role or performance of another individual.

Allport listed more than fifty definitions or meanings to the word personality. It has been defined as the "sum total and arrangement of psychological qualities," or as "the ability to adjust to environment." We might broaden our definition to include a sum total of the individual's qualities unique to him and distinguishing him from every other individual. We might categorize the sum total of all of these qualities as follows:

1. Physical: appearance — height, weight, age, race, or such things as the amount or style of hair, general health and neatness.
2. Intelligence — natural abilities and acquired knowledge and aptitudes.
3. Social — adjustment to situations and interaction with others.
4. Cultural — speech, bearing and poise, manner, creativity and attitude toward the aesthetic appreciation.
5. Moral — reputation, character and spiritual maturity.
6. Psychological — emotional stability and ability to cope with life's problems.

The personality of an individual includes his interests, sentiments, attitudes, feelings, values, temperaments, phobias, complexes, prejudices, motives, favored activities, and general habits. It is very difficult to find a "standard" definition of personality. Ryckman pointed out this problem:

> Despite the universal and eternal appeal of studying and understanding human personality, there is as yet no simple, integrated, and systematic theory of personality that provides a set of valid explanations to account for individual differences in behavior. Instead, there are almost as many definitions of personality as there are investigators in the discipline. . . .
>
> Despite the plethora of definitions, there is some basic agreement among investigators that personality is a hypothetical construct, that is, it is an abstraction which refers to an internal, *mediating* state of the individual. This state includes the person's unique learning history and biological propensities and the ways in which these organized complexes of events influence his or her reponses to certain stimuli in the environment. Thus, personality is seen by many investigators as the scientific study of individual differences in thought and behavior that occur under given situational circumstances. It also involves the similarities between individuals in thought and behavior that occur under different situational circumstances. Thus, providing explanations buttressed eventually by empirical evidence, for each individual's unique ways of responding to his environment.[10]

The common agreement among all the definitions and explanations of the social psychologists is that every person is unique — or a composition of a different set of personality traits, and that these traits are developed and demonstrated in the varied complex social systems when the person interacts with others, as stated by Smelser:

> The study of personality focuses on the individual as a system of needs, feelings, aptitudes, skills, defenses etc., or on one or more processes, such as the learning of skills. . . . The study of *social systems* focuses on certain relations that emerge when two or more persons interact with one another. . . .
>
> Conceptualizations of both personality and social systems are based on inferences from a common body of behavioral data — complex variety of phenomena; verbal and nonverbal communications, expressive movements, physiological states, interactions etc.[11]

TRAITS OF PERSONALITY

In his studies, Gordon Allport identified 18,000 words that describe some aspect or trait of human behavior. He grouped these words into three groups: Cardinal dispositions — those traits that dominate a person's entire existence; central dispositions — small number of traits that happen to be highly characteristic of a person; and secondary dispositions — traits that operate in limited situations.[12]

Trait descriptions often lead to overgeneralizations about an individual's characteristics. Another problem in ascribing to an individual certain personality traits is the fact that these traits often change at different times and places and under different situations, as well as appear in varying degrees. A person can exhibit one set of characteristics in the classroom — dignity and authority; in church — reverence and seriousness; at a gathering of friends — bubbling over with mirth. At a promotional meeting one might be enthusiastic and talkative, or in the office, quiet and diligent. When we describe someone's behavior we need to specify in what social situation these traits are to be found. A person who may present an outward impression of being cheerful and even light-hearted, may, in fact, inwardly be shy, morose, or despondent.

Each person is really an individual package of traits that cannot be measured accurately to the point of stereotyping him or her completely. I have categorized and briefly elaborated on just a few of the more dominant personality traits which are more readily recognizable:

1. *Traits that concern themselves with moral conduct* — honest or dishonest; truthful and sincere or deceptive and fraudulent; trustworthy, reliable, dependable or untrustworthy, etc.

2. *Mental attitudes toward life in general* — genial, kind, cordial, jovial or unkind, grouchy; happy, content, optomistic or morose, gloomy, moody, despondent, depressed; exuberant, vivacious or boring, dull.

3. *Traits demonstrated in dealing with others* — sociable, extrovert or unsociable, introvert; sympathetic or unsympathetic; unselfish and selfless or selfish, egotistical, conceited; cooperative or domineering, authoritarian; consistent or fickle, inconsistent, changeable.

4. *Traits that surface during unusual stress* — serene, calm or anger, rage, highly emotional; tolerance or frustration.

5. *Traits relating to financial situations* — generous, liberal or stingy,

avaricious; fair, considerate, or shrewd and scheming.

6. *Traits apparent during times of decision making* — sensible, wise, rational and logical or illogical, irrational, prejudiced, unduly biased or concerned, involved; apathetic and indifference.

In the analysis of The Teacher Characteristics Study, three patterns of teacher behavior stood out in separate factor analyses of observable data:

Pattern X — warm, understanding, friendly versus aloof, egocentric, restricted teacher behavior.

Pattern Y — responsible, businesslike, systematic versus evading, unplanned, slipshod teacher behavior.

Pattern Z — stimulating, imaginative, creative versus dull, routine teacher behavior.[13]

IDENTIFYING AND MEASURING PERSONALITY

Warga set down the following eight criteria for identifying normal and acceptable personality:

1. Behaves according to accepted social standards
2. Controls his or her emotions
3. Fulfils his or her human potential
4. Conforms to social customs
5. Is able to recognize consequences and thus guide his or her behavior
6. Can postpone immediate gratification to achieve long-range goals
7. Learns from experience
8. Is usually happy[14]

When we talk about a normal personality, we assume that there is a standard behavior. One can be somewhat to the right or left of this and still be considered normal. Warga listed the following ten traits which characterizes a well-adjusted individual:

1. Treats others as individuals
2. Works at full potential
3. Is productive in society
4. Can enjoy many things

5. Can resolve external stress
6. Can resolve internal stress
7. Identifies with other people, accepts and understands them whether liking them or not
8. Gets things done
9. Is not emotionally disturbed by stress
10. Has a native curiosity to find out and know about things[15]

This does not mean that a well-adjusted person must be a conformist. In dress, hair style, demeanor, conduct, bearing or behavior each individual should be himself and have a distinct personality. After all, as stated earlier, the personality of an individual consists of the specific organization of those traits that determine his or her uniqueness and the reactions to everything around himself.

A normal "healthy" personality refers to a person whose self-concept of his or her own traits is closely congruent with what others perceive these personality traits to be. Our perception of ourselves determines how we act. When the feedback we get from others conflicts with what we think of ourselves, instead of changing our ideas and perception of ourselves, we tend to distort the feedback so that the feedback is not inconsistent with the self-concept and thus continues to fit this false self-image. Concerning this human trait Warga wrote:

> Unfortunately, because the self-concept is not easy to change, this is an all too common way of absorbing inconsistent feedback. People who have spent their whole lives accumulating and filing evidence about themselves into some sort of logical pattern are usually not willing to make a drastic change in their personal evaluations very quickly, unless the feedback comes in massive doses. Even then, some people may crack under the stress of the inconsistent information rather than accept it.[16]

HOW PERSONALITY IS REVEALED

Since personality encompasses one's interests, feelings, attitudes, etc., how is an instructor most likely to divulge these to the students in the classroom and elsewhere? Personality reveals itself in a variety of ways — in dress, gait, posture, and the general way one goes about his work, relationships with other people, and through one's

emotional reactions to various situations. But one of
teacher displays personality traits is through speech; tʃ
choice of words, and the nonverbal, inflections of voiᳵ, ᵍᳵᵗᵗᵘᵗᵗᵉᵗ,
etc. Every time a person opens his mouth to speak he reveals at least
a portion of his personality. Just as our speech promptly reveals our
intelligence or lack of it — in other words, *what we know* — so speech
discloses our personality, or *who we are*. We might say that speech is
an index of what we really are and is the chief way of expressing our
personality. It has been referred to as "the mirror of one's soul." It is
the product of the entire person and an intricate part of one's adjustment to society.

It does not require a very great amount of speaking for us to categorize a person intellectually, culturally, or socially. In fact, in most
instances, before an individual in any type of a speaking situation
has completed the introduction, the listeners have concluded
whether the one who is talking really has anything worth listening to
and whether they should really bother to pay attention to what is being said from then on. During the opening sentences the one who is
speaking must create good will between himself and the members of
his audience. He must sell himself and reveal an acceptable personality.

The mass media of communication (radio and television) have
made the listeners voice conscious as well as language conscious.
The educated and uneducated alike are inclined to classify individuals intellectually, culturally, and socially by the way they speak. By
the time the prospective teacher goes to college there is seldom any
consciousness of how one sounds to others. He has grown up in a
community in which certain phonetic responses are used and understood. One's speech is taken for granted, and it has become a definite
and inseparable part of the personality. Monotony of voice results in
a boring teacher who is, no doubt bored with self and life in general
(at least bored with the subject being taught).

Teaching is not merely an intellectual matter. One cannot teach a
subject without projecting some kind of an attitude and feeling toward it and the hearers. The college and university teacher is not
some kind of communication apparatus who merely has a supply of
information and knowledge that he has assimilated and then cranks
out to whoever happens to care to receive it. Communication in the

teaching and learning processes involves a personal relationship between teacher and student. Personality is a very personal and individualized entity, and since one's speech and manners reveal this individual personality, so teaching styles vary with the personality of each teacher.

PROPER USE OF PERSONALITY IN TEACHING

It is impossible to ignore the personality factor in teaching. A professor or lecturer does not simply speak. He must speak in a certain characteristic way, displaying attitudes and personal feelings. It is very difficult for an instructor to cover up the true feelings about his or her work, subject, or students day after day for a portion or the entirety of an academic year or longer. Although some salespersons have perfected the art of deception, insincerity can sooner or later be detected by some little act or gesture and expression or simply the momentary tone of voice, as a result of which confidence is destroyed and communication is aborted.

The beginning college teacher should not try to emulate or imitate the style and personality of another teacher but develop his own style of teaching. Even among the professionals in the field of drama and the theater, it is very difficult to camouflage completely the real self and impersonate or imitate traits belonging to another. Whenever this is attempted in a prolonged situation as in the classroom, the listeners sense an element of insincerity, such as is often detected in commercials which frequently lack genuineness.

There are two undesirable extremes to which end the teacher may use or misuse personality. On the one hand, a teacher may strive to become a striking figure possessing a magnetic, winning, even irresistible personality, in which case the ever-present temptation to exploit the students by manipulating their feelings and behavior may lead to a desire for self-exaltation and "hero worship." On the other hand, a teacher may not really take personal interest in the presentation of the subject material, because he feels that personality should be kept out of teaching and that it is primarily the student's responsibility to acquire what he can of the knowledge being handed out.

Somewhere between these two extremes lies the proper employment of one's personality and one's self in the relationships between learning source and learner.

LACK OF CONVICTION AND DEDICATION

Related to the matter of personality, but not identical to it is the conviction and dedication of the college and university teacher. Without this necessary ingredient, classroom communication will suffer. A teacher must view his task as a service to mankind. If the influence of classroom interaction upon learning is to be a positive one, the instructor must be totally dedicated to the responsibilities inherent in the teaching profession.

MOTIVES FOR TEACHING

A teacher should love his work and teach with a sense of commitment and dedication. It is possible that certain aspects of the teaching profession, such as social and financial considerations prompt an individual to select it as a career. There exists a certain amount of security for the professor, especially if tenure has been acquired. There is still a degree of respect and prestige in achieving rank in an institution of higher education. The adage "the teacher is king in the classroom" still appeals to some persons who might feel that the competition in the business world or general society might deny them such authority.

These attitudes and motives, however, do not create the classroom climate or environment that is most apt to foster a free flow of ideas, but rather constitute hindrances and obstructions to communication. George Setterfield emphasized the fact that unless an instructor really wants to teach and enjoys teaching, any other motive that prompts anyone to become and remain in the profession reveals dishonesty and will affect rapport, and, consequently, communication in the classroom.

> Most intellectual pursuits are concerned with revealing or experiencing truth and as a result are closely bound up with honesty. . . . One es-

sential element of teaching depends on a subtle projection of the teacher's personal characteristics and nothing is more injurious to this subjective process than insincerity or falseness. Students in reacting to the teacher can sense such negative qualities almost immediately and although they may not be able to analyse precisely what is wrong they know that something is, and as a consequence rapport is lost. With rapport gone, with distrust or even hostility aroused, the teaching operation is reduced to a struggle to sell shoes to a wary buyer. . . .

Apart from the act of teaching, honesty must also be present in the motivations of the teacher. Basically he must teach because he really wants to teach. If a person merely teaches to earn time in the research lab or because it offers material advantages I find it unlikely that he will be more than a technically competent communicator.[17]

Every teacher knows when an honest, conscientious effort is being put forth in teaching a subject. The students also are keenly observant and aware of this. Without this commitment and dedication the work of teaching sooner or later becomes boring and distasteful and communication between teacher and students breaks down.

INTEREST IN STUDENTS

If a teacher derives pleasure and enjoyment from teaching it is probably a good indication that he likes other people, primarily the students, and respects them. There are many instructors, however, who do not seem to have any real personal interest in their students as evidenced by the fact that they hardly look up at them at all as they monotonously read their lecture notes and appear to be completely detached from the members of their audience. Generally they are inaccessible to their students (in the classroom as well as out of it) as they live their own private lives. It is possible that a teacher may not know much more about his students as individuals at the end of the term than at the beginning. I remember one large undergraduate class that I attended in which the professor had a seating chart with the names of all the class members but never bothered to learn to whom any of the names belonged. In addressing specific students occasionally he would look at them and say, "Hey, you."

Dan Wolf suggests that we who teach can learn from business and recognize what business discovered in the Hawthorne plant research at the Western Electric Company, namely, that production and morale can be increased when the workers feel that management is interested in them as individuals. "If the principle is sound for business," he said, "is it not reasonable to assume that student morale and academic output might increase if students felt their professors were interested in them as individuals?" One basic way of showing interest is in recognizing a person's name. "In a business where supervisors and other management representatives can acknowledge employees by name, overall worker morale is boosted. The individual gains some assurance that the company is interested in him as a person."[18] As has been suggested, every teacher should put forth a determined effort to learn the names of the students in his class and associate the names with faces, and in every way possible take a personal interest in them.

This commonsense philosophy has been successfully demonstrated not only in the business world but in every other area where relationships between people exists. In August of 1943 when Mountbatten took up his new appointment he had a very difficult task to perform in Southeast Asia. His first offensive was to restore the morale of his men, which was at a very low ebb. He fought the attitude of apathy and defeatism at every level and instilled an entirely new spirit and philosophy of fighting. He got his men around him and said, "I hear you call this the Forgotten Front, I hear you call yourselves the Forgotten Army. Well, let me tell you that this is not the Forgotten Front, and you are not the Forgotten Army. In fact, nobody has even heard of you. But they will hear of you because this is what we are going to do. . . ." It was not long until his men began to feel that people actually cared about them and this heightened their morale.

This personal interest which changed people's lives can be seen earlier in his career when the ship he commanded was sunk by the Germans and half the crew was lost, Mountbatten told the surviving members, "There isn't one of you that I wouldn't be proud and honoured to serve with again. Goodbye, good luck, and thank you all from the bottom of my heart." "It is a measure of the special morale of the *Kelly* that today, forty years since she went to the bottom, the Reunion Association is as active as ever — the only one of its kind run by the survivors of a destroyed ship's company."[19] This is perhaps the greatest tribute of all of Mountbatten's leadership.

It is important for the teacher to understand people and be genuinely interested in them as well as to understand his own subject material. College and university teaching should be viewed as a highly personal and responsible assignment, which demands great intellectual and moral qualities in the relationships and exchange of ideas between professor and students. McKeachie expressed this relationship as follows:

> What are the satisfactions in teaching? Certainly one is the pleasure of seeing a student develop. Another is the pleasure of intellectual interchange with young people possessing questioning minds and fresh ideas. Perhaps a less laudable but nonetheless real satisfaction is that found in having disciples who respect us. These satisfactions are difficult to secure without close, sustained personal contact with students. . . .
>
> Enjoyment of teaching is important not only for the enthusiasm which the professor communicates to his students but also for his interest in continued improvement. These important values are likely to be lost if teaching becomes so routinized and depersonalized that it is no longer fun.[20]

NOTES

1. Getzels, J.W., and Jackson, P.W.: The teacher's personality and characteristics. In Gage, N.L. (Ed.): *Handbook of Reseach on Teaching.* Chicago, Rand McNally and Co., 1963, p. 506.
2. Rees, Richard: Dimensions of students' points of view in rating college teachers, *Journal of Educational Psychology, 60*:476, 1969.
3. Morton, Richard K.: Personal background of effective teaching. *Improving College and University Teaching, 8*:137, 1960.
4. Morton, Richard K.: Personal background of effective teaching, p. 136.
5. Glicksberg, Charles I.: What makes a classroom. *Improving College and University Teaching, 5, No. 2*:69, 1957.
6. Morton, Richard K.: Learning as communication. *Improving College and University Teaching, 19*:144, 1971.
7. Getzels, J.W., and Jackson, P.W.: The teacher's personality and characteristics. pp. 566, 567.
8. Williams, Reed G., and Ware, John E., Jr.: Validity of student ratings of instruction under different incentive conditions: a further study of the Dr. Fox effect. *Journal of Educational Psychology, 68, No. 1*:48, 50, February, 1976.
9. Coats, William D., and Smidchens, Uldis: Audience recall as a function of speaker dynamism. *Journal of Educational Psychology, 57, No. 4*:189, August,

1966.

10. Ryckman, Richard M.: *Theories of Personality.* New York, D. Van Nostrand Co., 1978, pp. 3, 4.

11. Smelser, Neil J., and Smelser, William T.: *Personality and Social Systems.* New York, John Wiley and Sons, Inc., 1963, pp. 3, 4.

12. Warga, Richard G.: *A Psychology of Personal Adjustment.* 2nd ed. Boston, Houghton-Mifflin Co., 1979. (See Chapter 1, quoting Allport).

13. Getzels, J.W., and Jackson, P.W.: The teacher's personality and characteristics. p. 567.

14. Warga, Richard: *A Psychology of Personal Adjustment* p. 7.

15. Warga, Richard: *A Psychology of Personal Adjustment* p. 19.

16. Warga, Richard: *A Psychology of Personal Adjustment* p. 81.

17. Setterfield, George: Elements of creativity in teaching. In Sheffield, Edward F. (Ed.): *Teaching in the Universities: No One Way.* Montreal, McGill-Queen's University Press, 1974, pp. 44, 45.

18. Wolf, Dan B.: Can education learn from business? *Improving College and University Teaching, 13, No. 2*:110, Spring, 1965.

19. Hough, Richard: *Mountbatten, Hero of Our Time.* London, Weidenfeld and Nicolson, 1980, pp. 135, 178.

20. McKeachie, W.J.: Research on teaching at the college and university level. In Gage, N.L. (Ed.): *Handbook of Research on Teaching.* Chicago, Rand McNally and Co., 1963, pp. 1163, 1164.

Part III
TEACHING METHODS
Classroom Presentation

CHAPTER 4

PROPER TEACHING METHODS

A great lecture is as significant as a brilliant symphony.
When it touches the hearts and the imagination of students it
has a lasting value. . . . An inspired lecturer gives color to
experience; he heightens the sensations of the moment.
Students thus experience what Aristotle calls a catharsis, a
projection of individuality into a universal realm.

Frederick Mayer

PART II dealt with the intellectual, social, and emotional
development (and background) of the prospective teacher in the
preparation for a lifetime performance in the professional career of
teaching, with an emphasis upon those areas where deficiencies
often exist which may later result in partial or complete blockage of
the communication process. Throughout the entire period of
teaching, indeed, throughout the whole life span one should broaden
the educational horizons and ever strive to reach levels of potential
maturity intellectually, socially and emotionally. This continual
growth should lead to a greater degree of effective communication
and rapport.

Part III deals with various techniques and methods, and the
understanding and use of rhetorical and psychological principles
necessary as vehicles of teaching and learning in classroom
communication. This chapter focuses on teaching methods and how

they affect communication of information and concepts from source to receiver. Classroom communication can break down, not only by the ineffective use of the best method for a particular course of study, but in the employment of the *wrong* teaching method.

The lack of effective communication in teaching is often blamed on the teaching *method* used in the classroom, rather than on the *abuse* of that method by an inefficient or untrained instructor. In this chapter I wish to show how, in spite of the fact that admittedly one method of teaching may have some advantages over another technique under certain varying circumstances (such as the nature of the subject, size of the class, level of the course — lower or upper division or graduate course, aim or objective perceived by the professor), often the ineffectiveness of communication actually lies in the execution of a method and can be traced to the faults and deficiencies of the teacher, rather than some inherent alleged weakness of a given method.

CRITICISMS OF THE LECTURE METHOD

The first and foremost teaching method to be considered is the lecture. It has been and continues to be the most widely used method of classroom communication. It also has been and continues to be the most criticized, maligned, and condemned by teachers and students of all the methods available to university and college teaching. A great number of articles and several complete books have been written during the past four decades by both critic and defender in either attacking the lecture method and demanding its demise or in extolling its virtues and pleading for its continued existence and intelligent usage. Many controlled (and some not so carefully monitored) experiments have been conducted during this same period of time on both sides of the Atlantic, in an effort to determine which method of teaching is the most effective in view of the objectives sought.

"Don't lecture to me!" has taken on the same antagonistic connotation as the oft-repeated phrase (or denunciation), "Don't preach to me!" and to a great extent because of the same psychological and rhetorical faults. Over and over again we have been, and still are be-

ing told, that the lecture was outmoded by the invention of the printing press and easy availability of printed material, referring to the
oft-quoted statement by Boswell in *Life of Johnson* (p. 181), "Lectures
were once useful; but now, when all can read, and books are so numerous, lectures are unnecessary. If your attention fails, and you
miss part of a lecture, it is lost; you cannot go back as you can upon
a book."

Len Powell, in the beginning of his book, *Lecturing,* implies that
after listening to all the "evidence" brought by teachers and researchers against the lecture method, and as a result of the feelings of re-
sentfulness on the part of those who are daily subjected to lecturing
— the students, "there are good reasons for reviewing the role of the
lecturer as means of communication."[1] Since this present book deals
primarily with communication breakdown in college and university
lecturing, it is indeed essential to look carefully at the problems relative to the lecture method in order to decide whether it can be effectively employed for general classroom communication.

ATTITUDE OF ADMINISTRATORS AND PROFESSORS
ABOUT LECTURES

Powell summarized the criticisms of the lecture into three general
areas: (1) pedagogical, (2) psychological, and (3) sociological. Let us
first consider some of the criticisms that relate to the pedagogical.
How do many of the educators feel about the value and use of lectures? One of the main objections seems to be that lecturing is a
monologue, in which the professor does all the talking, and the students are involved only in passive participation; consequently, get
only a one-sided view of the subject and, as Powell expressed it,
"physical passivity of listeners promotes a false sense of security and
represses initiatives."[2] I personally knew a teacher who daily read
very rapidly from his notes from the very start of the class period until five minutes after the closing bell, while the more energetic students furiously scribbled down in their notes what they could catch
of the lecture material. There was never time to listen, to think and
meditate, or to ask questions.

Lecture — A One-way Communication

This accusation that the lecture is a monologue or one-way communication in which the lecturer is uninformed by any verbal feedback, is so serious that its discontinuance has been advocated by educators. Such feelings were expressed in an article entitled, "An Assessment of the Lecture:"

> This study was undertaken because of a subjective feeling that the value of the lecture as a method of conveying information has limitations serious enough to warrant its discontinuance in our courses. Not the least of these limitations is that the lecture is a monolog, a one way discourse which either does not allow or minimizes student participation. Such a condition is actually at odds with the fundamental instructional principle that learning is maximized or facilitated if the learner participated or interacts with the teacher."[3]

In the editorial column of the journal, *Improving College and University Teaching,* there appeared a brief article entitled, "A Talking Teacher Cannot Succeed," in which the following comment was made: "If talking were teaching, then students might thrive. We talk a lot, calling it 'lecturing,' but do our students thrive?" Reference was then made to one of these "talking teachers" in whose class session "a bold student who ventured an opinion or question got short shrift, for the professor has his lecture to 'cover'. His teaching was about as stimulating as week-old pancake batter; there was no 'rise' in it, no response, no 'feedback'."[4]

Lectures Often Read in Monotone

Related to the first main objection — that the teacher is merely a one-way performer — comes the added charge that, not only does the teacher monopolize the talking, but often his talking is done in connection with the reading of a script, and poor reading at that. The natural consequence of this objection to the lecture then is that lectures are monotonous, dull, and boring. When derogatory remarks are made verbally or appear in print about lecturing, it is assumed by the spokesman or writer of such statements that lectures are of necessity dull, boring, tedious, and frightfully uninteresting because they are so often read in a monotone fashion. The previously mentioned editorial cited a typical "talking teacher" who would come shambling into class, spread his notes, and for fifty minutes read in a monotone and then depart.

This matter of dull, monontous reading of outdated scripts seems to delight those caricaturing opponents of the lecture method, most of whom appear to take it for granted that this is inherent to the lecture, rather than being a senseless abuse of the lecture by the performer. This attitude has been with us for a number of decades. In an article entitled, "Is Lecturing Teaching?" Charles Glicksberg wrote:

> The lecture system often bogs down badly when the professor proceeds to read directly from his lecture notes, generally notes that have been preserved for years. . . . The teacher clearly understood what he was talking about, but he was not communicating his knowledge to the class. . . . The lecturer often adheres too rigorously and too monotonously to the officially prescribed text. . . . Frequently the lecture is uninteresting, since the instructor presents stale ideas in a soporifically monotonous tone. . . . The result is not only lack of interest but downright boredom. Too many lecturers do a good job of anaesthetizing their audience. The students have difficulty suppressing their yawns.[5]

Glicksberg referred to what many students have been subjected to in lectures as "the purgatory of boredom."

Lectures Often Duplicate Material in Textbooks

Another charge levelled against the lecture is that there is a tendency to repeat information that students can get in more lucid form in textbooks. The editorial, "A Talking Teacher Cannot Succeed" referred to the *talking teacher* in lecturing who "said nothing that wasn't in the textbooks, and the textbooks said nothing he didn't."[6] This accusation implies that the lecturer sticks too close to the text and wastes time that could better be spent in reading or that he belabors the obvious and often is not prepared to answer questions dealing with material not covered in the textbook.

Glicksberg also alluded to this criticism when he cited the example of the "professor who read his lecture notes slavishly," and thereby "gave the unmistakable impression that he did not know his subject matter thoroughly. . . . He did not take the trouble to explain the technical terms he used. . . . Often the students ask him to explain what he has said. Instead of explaining, he repeats the statement."[7]

(quoting the students) "We still fail to understand the meaning but he continues his reading. If we ask him questions that are not in the text, he usually asks a student to answer. If the student is correct, we benefit; if he is incorrect, we are told to forget about it."[7]

Lecturing is Ineffective for Most Types of Learning

Educators tell us that if lecturing has any legitimacy at all, it might be used for the purpose of presenting factual information, but that it is ineffective for the more important and challenging objectives. In fact, it is supposedly no more effective than other methods even for this purpose of transfer of information and knowledge.

> We have seen that lectures are relatively ineffective to teach students to think about a topic and have doubtful effectiveness in developing attitudes and values. . . . Problem-centered lectures are the most difficult to give and require extremely careful preparation of the inter-relation of the subject matter.[8]

Many other charges are made against the lecture, such as it is too remote or not related to students' needs, or that it is too formal, too rigid, or, on the other hand, too superficial and lacking in preparation and organization, and also that often it is delivered too rapidly — all of which result in frustration on the part of the students who, because of these apparent weaknesses and limitations consider the lecture "a waste of time."

Besides these pedagogical objections raised by educators to lecturing, the long list of criticisms also includes allegedly psychological effects of the lecture. The lecturer is said to maintain a psychological advantage by the authority or intellectual position, as well as by the physical position of standing in front of the students, who are seated in rows facing the teacher, thus creating a tendency for the lecturer to exaggerate and the audience to pose or submit. The result of these relationships supposedly causes an "imbalance of psychological superiority," which tends "to promote insincerity."

We are also told that the lecture method tends to create a sociological effect in that small group bondings are repressed, which makes individuals feel isolated, or that the lecture stifles the desire for self-expression instead of promoting it, and thereby disregarding the natural desire for social interaction, especially with one's peers.

Worse than this is the accusation that the "climate" in the lecture hall continues to be cold and completely impersonal.

STUDENT OPINIONS REGARDING LECTURES

According to the opinions expressed by students both in America and Great Britain, the effects of the lecture method as described previously have left the recipients very dissatisfied and disgruntled. One student voiced his opinion in a student forum as follows: "The lecture system must be abolished in American teaching because it allows no flexibility in pattern for student question. . . . In the best interest of American higher education the lecture system must be abolished."[9]

Glicksberg quoted students' comments concerning lectures in these appraisals:

> The lecturer is like a robot who continues to perform his task whether or not anyone is benefiting from his actions. The bell starts him off and then stops him. The professor does not seem to be aware that his audience consists of human beings who need time to absorb information and to discuss it. The lecturer could very easily be replaced by a recording of the information.[10]

One student cuttingly defined the lecture system as "an unending drone of meaningless words spoken in a meaningless monotone." Besides these random selections of student reactions to lectures in American colleges and universities, we have a general student attitude to the lecture method in Great Britain compiled by David Mollet, Senior Lecturer in Philosophy of Education at the School of Education at Preston Polytechnic. He sent out questionnaires to 112 students of philosophy of education at the close of the 1974-75 academic year. These students were asked to evaluate the different teaching methods with reference to the imparting and transmission of a body of knowledge, and the means whereby the students develop an understanding of the subject matter. The students indicated that even though the lecture was an acceptable method in communicating a body of knowledge, independent study and tutorials were rated higher.

Furthermore the questionnaire revealed that the students regarded the lecture method as the least efficient way of developing an understanding of the subject.[11]

HOW EXPERIMENTS RATE LECTURES

Thus far in this chapter all of the categories of criticism against the lecture have been drawn from the observations, personal experience, opinions, and prejudices of educators and students. Can these accusations and evaluations of the lecture be verified by experimentation and research? The staff of the University Teaching Unit of London University encourages us to rely upon scientific studies rather than on our own likes and dislikes. We are warned against reacting to our own prejudices and reminded that empirical evidence is usually more trustworthy.[12]

Even though some research has been conducted for many years in an effort to determine the strengths and weaknesses of various teaching techniques, in recent years educational literature has been inundated with results of experiments and studies on both sides of the Atlantic. It would be too redundant (and somewhat tedious) to consider all of these experiments here. I wish, however, carefully to examine some of these studies and allude to a number of others in an attempt, first of all, to see what conclusions were reached, and second, to briefly test the validity of some of these experiments.

To begin with, I would like to refer to a well-known and oft-quoted experiment conducted by Dr. John McLeish, published by the Cambridge Institute of Education. In an introductory note to McLeish's book, *The Lecture Method*, Robert H. Thouless (M.A., Ph.D., Sc.D.) stated that "questions about the value of the lecture are not new. What is new is the manner of getting answers to them by experimental enquiry instead of by argument. There are many questions to *be* answered." The first of such questions that he believed needs an answer was, "Is the lecture, as commonly delivered, an effective way of conveying the kind of information required at university level?" Thouless wrote that the usefulness, of the lecture, which has had a long history as the central method of university instruction, has been "so much taken for granted that it may seem to many to be almost blasphemous to doubt its value." He predicted, however, that "the university of the future may not include the activity of lecturing at all."[13]

The Norwich Experiment

One of the better-known experiments conducted by McLeish is the one carried out in Norwich, Norfolk, England. Concerning this Norwich experiment, McLeish stated the main experimental objective was to determine how much information students were able to get in their notes and remember for recall in an examination of material delivered in a given lecture. The students who volunteered were instructed to take notes on the lecture, just as they would in their own classroom lectures, and be prepared to answer test questions after the lecture. A summary of the lecture was written on the blackboard as well. The subject of the lecture in this experiment was a comparison of the theories of child development of Freud, Piaget, and Parsons, demonstrating their common origin in the views of Charles Darwin. The students who volunteered for this experiment had no previous knowledge of these theories.

From McLeish's description of his experiment, it is not clear whether some of the students heard the lecture live, but it is clear that a number of them heard it played back to them on a tape recorder. Some purposely heard only a portion of the lecture. When tested on the material, it was found that only about 42 percent of the information was remembered and jotted down in notes immediately after hearing the lecture, and after a week another test was administered, which indicated that the students could not recall half of that 42 percent of the material originally remembered.[14]

Trenaman's Experiments

McLeish built his experiments on those of the pioneer work of Joseph Trenaman, who claimed that the spoken word generally failed to communicate anything at all after the first fifteen minutes. Trenaman's experiments consisted of playing back recordings of forty-five minute broadcast talks by distinguished speakers. The volunteers who heard one of these talks on astronomy by Professor Fred Hoyle were apparently students from an astronomy class but seemed to range widely in age and educational level. Some heard only fifteen minutes, some listened for thirty minutes, and others heard the entire forty-five minute talk. All were immediately tested on that portion of the talk that they had heard. In general those who heard only the first fifteen minutes scored an immediate recall of 41 percent of the information. Those who heard thirty minutes retained 25 percent, and those who listened to the entire recorded talk retained only 20 percent. A week later those who heard only the first fifteen minutes recalled twice as much as the ones who heard the whole talk. These results were explained in the following comments:

> With the increase in the duration of the talk the amount remembered thinned out. In the typical case, assimilation began to diminish seriously after 15 minutes. At 30 minutes, most listeners were approaching the point where the total they were taking in was zero. In some cases there was, in fact, a loss of material previously learned so that the total amount assimilated as time went on was continuously decreasing. This is, of course, the phenomenon known as retroactive inhibition, well-known to psychologists. It can be defined as the process whereby there is a forgetting, or loss of material previously learned, due to the working back on it of later learning.[15]

As a result of his own and the experiment of others like Trenaman, McLeish suggested that the oral methods such as the lecture are not especially effective for transmitting information and the understanding of principles or the application of these principles. He advocated more systematic investigation of the lecture method and other teaching techniques and added, "it is a wry testimonial to the entrenched position of the lecture system in higher education that Trenaman's work signally failed to trigger off any such empirical studies."[16]

Donald Bligh's Studies

One of the most often quoted and most extensive studies on the subject of teaching methods was conducted by Donald Bligh of the London University Teaching Method Unit and director of the Teaching Services Centre of the University of Exeter. His conclusions reached, as a result of a great deal of research, are incorporated in his book *What's the Use of Lectures* and other books and articles. The massive amounts of evidence employed seem so convincing that the conclusions are virtually assumed to be factual and nondebatable. Bligh compared all of the various teaching methods by applying each method to every possible aim and purpose of teaching and evaluated or equated each in one of the three alternative answers to measurements — more effective, less effective, or no significant difference. Bligh referred to Dubin and Taveggia who had reviewed ninety-one studies, comparing two or more teaching methods on one or more measures of "course content." To illustrate what I may be finding difficult to explain, Bligh compared the lecture method to every conceivable variation and combination or modification of the discussion, seminar, tutorial, and independent study, and categorized sixty-eight studies or experimental findings in three columns representing the three alternative conclusions listed previously. He came up with sixteen studies showing that the lecture was more effective; thirty-eight showed no significant difference; and fourteen indicated that lectures were less effective.

The previous listing refers only to lectures used for the *transfer of information*. A similar comparison was also made for the purpose of *promotion of thought*, with the general conclusion that lectures are relatively ineffective to stimulate thought. Yet another categorization was produced in the same three areas of being more effective, less effective, or no significantly difference in cases where the teacher's or subject's objective was that of *changing attitudes*, and again Bligh concluded that lectures are relatively ineffective.

It is very difficult to see how all of this vast, almost overwhelming amount of research could be digested and how anyone could come up with a simple generalization as Bligh did in his final conclusion that "although it is sometimes believed that the lecture method can fulfill three kinds of function the available evidence suggests that it can only effectively achieve one — the students' acquisition of information." He added that if the lecturers wished to achieve other objectives they had better use other methods.[17]

Even for the purpose of transmitting information Bligh did not favor the lecture all that much in the first of three general principles upon which he based his book. (1) "The lecture is as effective as any other method for transmitting information, but not more effective." The other two generalizations about the lecture are even much less favorable. (2) "Most lectures are not as effective as more active methods for the promotion of thought," and (3) "Changing student attitudes should not normally be the major objective of a lecture." Bligh did, however, justify his writing a book about how to prepare and present lectures on the presumption that "administrative, economic or other considerations may force their use for the promotion of thought or attitudes," in spite his warning that "lectures should not be accepted as the normal vehicle for this kind of teaching."[18]

Bligh and others from the University Teaching Unit (G.J. Ebrahim, David Jaques and D. Warren Piper), as a result of all the available evidence, attached the following six *limitations to the lecture method,* and suggest that even when used for the appropriate purpose of transfer of information, the lecture method should be combined with other methods: (1) Students' perceptions of what is said are normally inaccurate, as judged by the notes they take, because their previous understanding of the subject is necessarily limited. (2) Memory of information presented fades very rapidly at first and more slowly later. (They cited a study by Jones back in 1923, in which it was found that students' memory of information faded from 60% immediately after a lecture to 23% eight weeks later.) (3) "Lectures are linear in form . . . providing a framework for a subject. . . . But if the students do not already possess a framework of relevant ideas, the linear form of the lecture is quite inappropriate to teach it." (Whereas in reading a book the reader can proceed at his own rate of understanding and go back over the material that he did not at first comprehend.) (4) There is a declining student attention during the lecture. From the results of four studies, Thomas (1972), Lloyd (1968), and Bligh (1972, 1974), the conclusion was reached that the proportion of information retained during a lecture declines steadily after an initial settling-in period. This decline continues until near the end of an hour or nearly an hour lecture, at which time there seems to be a brief but sharp rise in attention. The evidence for these conclusions was taken from the students' notes and the recording of their heartbeats during the lecture period. (5) The lecturer obtains little immediate verbal feedback on his effectiveness. (Although it was admitted that there were other ways than merely verbal to evaluate feedback or student reactions, few lecturers feel it is their responsibility to observe these reactions.) (6) Lectures are relatively ineffective to teach students to think about a topic and have doubtful effectiveness in developing attitudes and values.[19]

EVALUATION OF CRITICISM AND "EVIDENCE" AGAINST LECTURES
Opinion of Educators

How valid are personal observations, arguments, and examples cited by teachers themselves against the lecture method of classroom teaching? Are these arguments prompted by facts in every instance or flavored by personal prejudices? Are the examples summoned against lecturing representative of the overall situation or highly selective in order to substantiate and support a preconceived judgment? Are these attitudes and opinions concerning the lecture merely indicative of some personal inadequacies to handle the lecture effectively? Finally, are these critics overlooking basic faults and weaknesses in the lecturers and their role in the education system, rather than in the lecture method itself? When it comes right down to it, it appears as though most of the arguments offered and examples cited point up the *abuses* of the lecture method rather than potentials within the lecture as a technique of teaching and classroom communication.

We have already seen in Chapters 2 and 3 that a lack of education and a lack of training in communicative skills, as well as a lack of acceptable personality, enthusiasm, and dedication can, and does, lead to a partial or even complete breakdown in classroom communication. Other areas of communication breakdown will be discussed in the chapters that follow. When communication breaks down for *any* of these many reasons, in *any* of the various methods of classroom teaching, it is obvious and natural that the method (and students) will likewise suffer to that degree. What these professors, who have "testified" against lecturing, are witnessing all about them are flagrant violations of psychological and rhetorical principles that greatly reduce the effectiveness of the lecture method regardless for what objective it is being employed, even when it is used for that purpose for which it is claimed best suited — the transfer of information and knowledge.

What kind of lecturers do Glicksberg and his fellow critics in the teaching profession select when they look at lecturing? Here are some of the characteristics of a *typical* lecturer (unfortunately, easy to locate on almost any college and university campus!) (1) The lecturer reads lecture notes, instead of presenting the subject material in an interesting, enthusiastic manner — extemporaneously, and putting all of his energies into what he is saying as well as keeping good eye-contact with his hearers. (2) The lecturer's outdated notes have been preserved for years, instead of keeping up with the latest developments in his field and making the lecture relevant to the students sitting in the class. (3) The lecturer gives the unmistakable impression to his students that he really does not know himself exactly what he is talking about, because he reads his lecture notes slavishly, instead of fluently presenting material from the vast store of knowledge in the subject area, so that the listening students will recognize his competence and respect him for his expertise. (4) The material throughout the "lecture" is not well-organized, and it is obvious to all who try to listen, if indeed there are those who still are doing so, that the lecturer either does not really know how to teach, or else simply did not bother to prepare adequately for the current day's presentation. Instead the teacher should have had all the material so well-organized that it is both interesting and easy to follow. The students should have the impression that they are taking a journey together and know where they are each step of the way and experience a feeling of satisfaction at the end of the lecture period that they have all reached their predetermined destination together. (5) The lecturer did not take the trouble to define and explain these *labels* or expressions and show the relationship of each to the topics under consideration. (6) The lecturer often adheres too rigorously and too monotonously to the officially prescribed text, either reading from the text or saying nothing that is not already in the textbook. Any unqualified person can stand before a class and merely *flip pages* in the textbook! The combination of reading the text or stale notes, and poorly at that, in a monotonous manner, devoid of a sense of humor — that is really depicting a dullard. Why did these critics not cite those who do a satisfactory job of supplementing the textbook with further explanation, examples and a bit of humor? (7) The atmosphere in the lecture hall remains completely impersonal, instead of the lecturer creating and developing rapport with each student in a relaxed environment. (8) In these examples cited by the critics, the lecturer not only reads in a monotonous voice but also reads too rapidly, so that the students scribble all they can recall as fast as they can, and at the end of the lecture hour find themselves completely exhausted. (9) The lecturer is an authoritative figure, carrying on a monologue and never providing any opportunity for student participation or caring about feedback, instead of showing an interest and concern for the individual student and encouraging interaction and exchange of ideas during or at the end of the lecture.

How can these professors justify the abandonment of the lecture method, just because there are many poor lecturers, who, in actuality, are not really lecturers at all but are unskilled blunderers in a perfectly legitimate educational activity. Perhaps the lecturers depicted by these professors loathe the subject they are teaching or even hate their students. Why blame all of these communication roadblocks of ignorance, apathy, or disinterest on the act of lecturing, as though these "qualities" were inherent in the system or are necessary traits that belong to this method of teaching? Any such insipid, tedious, unimaginative, lifeless performance in which the lecturer is insensible to the needs of the learner, and is unaware of the obligation to the tuition-paying students, simply is not lecturing.

Opinion of Students

Students know more about the classroom performance of the lecturer than do the members of the administration or fellow faculty and staff, because they are the ones who suffer most from poor lecturing (and benefit the most from good lecturing). Even though students may not have the training to qualify them to evaluate lectures, their reaction day by day to a teacher's performance (and by testing the amount of learning that has resulted) can verify the results of the weaknesses in classroom lecturing. As we shall see, however, in a later chapter dealing with listening skills, a part of the breakdown in the learning process is due to the students' poor study habits, note-taking techniques, lack of previous knowledge of the subject under discussion, inability to concentrate properly, low-level interest in the subject and simply low IQ.

In the comments made by students concerning teaching techniques, and from the results of the questionnaires filled out by students, we can judge that they are not evaluating the merits of the lecture so much as passing judgment on what is being handed to them in a particular method, and, consequently, if they are unfortunately subjected to such a poor lecturer as described in the testimonials of educators about lecturers, they are very quick to see the individual faults, and, therefore, condemn the entire system. If they are subjected to lecturers whose daily presentation is "an unending drone of meaningless words spoken in a meaningless monotone rendered in a boring voice of the professor who seems more interested in the subject than yourself," condemnation will be evoked upon the entire teaching method.

Student evaluations can serve as a benefieical and excellent form of classroom feedback, as pointed out on pages 196 and 197, where I cite Colin Flood Page's summarization of Remmer's list of advantages and disadvantages of student evaluations. Oral or written student evaluations, however, for the purposes of either judging the performances of the lecturers or evaluating lecturing as a teaching method cannot be heavily relied upon. The reliability of student evaluation can be affected by such subjective criteria as grades received, personal likes or dislikes of teachers, amount or complexity of assignments, interest in and difficulty of the subject, reputation of the instructor or prejudicial attitudes toward the lecturer. The opportunity to evaluate teachers may be used by some students as a chance to "strike back" at them. Because of these subjective elements, students may not be the best judges of the effectiveness of teachers as lecturers. They are, nevertheless, definitely in a much better position to determine whether teachers employ the lecture method effectively day by day, than they are to evaluate the inherent qualities of the lecture method itself.

Experimentation and Research

Is it possible to measure the effectiveness of the lecture method accurately by experiments when there are so many variables and so many inadequacies in using the scientific method of investigation to areas of human beavhior? There are many variants to be considered before drawing conclusions from experiments and studies, first, in connection with the students whose learning is being tested; second, factors relating to individual classroom situations; third, with the different purposes and objectives of a given course of instruction; fourth, with the performance of the individual lecturer; and, finally, variations possible within each method itself.

Let us consider some of the difficulties researchers encounter in attempts at controlling experiments to determine the amount of learning that takes place under certain conditions.

Variables Relating to The Students

SIZE OF THE CLASS. Bligh, McKeachie and others claim that in their experiments this element of class size did not make a significant difference in individual student learning. In a summary statement in the research done in America on the lecture method, McKeachie concluded that for the transfer of information, "lectures of large size are not generally inferior to smaller lecture classes if one uses traditional achievement tests. When other objectives are used (e.g. developing concepts, problem-solving skills, favorable attitudes to a subject) large lectures are on shakier ground but are not consistently inferior. However, both students and faculty members feel that teaching is more effective in small classes."[20]

Bligh and others claim the same results are seen in large as in small classes. "A world-wide problem is the large size of lecture classes. These are more difficult for lecturers to observe; but contrary to common opinion, available evidence (Bligh, 1972) does not suggest that they are less effective. Indeed, most investigations have found them slightly superior."[21]

There really is not much of a choice in large classes as to teaching method. How would it be possible to have a discussion group for 100 or 200 students, unless one day a week they met in many smaller groups, which would be very difficult for the instructor to handle? Even more impossible would be the seminar or tutorial with such great numbers. A much larger staff would be required to cope with so many.

AGE AND MATURITY OF THE STUDENT AND LEVEL OF STUDY. Independent study may fair better than lectures in an experiment that tests the learning on the graduate level rather than the lower division course in the undergraduate level.

STUDENT'S INTEREST IN AND PREVIOUS KNOWLEDGE OF THE SUBJECT. It is quite obvious that if a person has a definite initial interest in a particular subject and has already gained some information concerning this specific area, there will be a much greater likelihood that the lecture method, or any other method, will be much more effective than if there were no initial interest or even an aversion to the subject matter and, indeed, a general lack of knowledge relating to the subject area.

STUDENTS' MOTIVATION TO LEARN. A subject may be in the student's major area, and he will be more highly motivated to learn in order to pass course requirement and possible comprehensive examination. A student's personal interest will act as a stimulus to learning, especially if the material he is expected to learn in a given course is meaningful and has relevance to a future career.

Variables Relating to Individual Classroom Situations

NATURE OF THE SUBJECT. Some subjects lend themselves much more appropriately to one method than another. Not only is this true of certain subject areas, but also the emphasis placed by the instructor on a given course may vary, such as laying down broad principles or building up detailed knowledge on which these principles are based.

VARIABLES IN OUTSIDE ASSIGNMENTS. In lecture classes where the students are assigned *outside* reading, as well as the reading of the textbook, how can one measure the effectiveness of one method, when learning is rarely isolated to a single source or method.

Differences in Objectives of a Course

We have already noted the three categories of Bligh's studies, the acquisition of information, the promotion of thought, and changes in attitudes. Another way of stating these course objectives would be background knowledge of a subject problem-solving, and value judgment and understanding.

Differences in Lecturers

There are obvious differences in the intellectual, psychological and rhetorical limitations or qualities among lecturers. In the experiments a poor lecturer may be compared to a good discussion leader, for example. Teachers find unidentical results with individual students, and conversely, some students learn much more from some teachers than others, even when the teachers employ the same teaching method. In fact, so complicated are the variables that it is possible for the same teacher to get varying results with the same students at different times, in spite of the fact that the same teaching method is used.

The Same Method Differs Considerably

The details of a teaching method may vary. For example, one lecturer may write out his lecture verbatim and read his script in a formal or impersonal manner with scarcely any indications of awareness of having an audience. On the other hand, another lecturer could speak very informally and be carrying on a *conversation* with his listeners, during which time there exists much physical feedback in student reactions and some oral response. There might actually be only a short step between this latter type of lecture and the discussion. The discussion method might also vary greatly. In one instance the teacher could act as chairperson or moderator and keep strictly to his outline, or the discussion could be a nondirective, free group buzz session.

Research Findings Vary Enormously

Researchers sometimes come up with completely conflicting conclusions. According to one set of experiments we are told that a certain teaching method is more effective for a particular teaching objective, but the results of another researcher's studies indicate that another method would be far more efficient, and yet both sources of information claim scientific procedures in arriving at their conclusions.

Validating the Evidence Against Lectures

As pointed out in an article entitled, "The Lecture Effectiveness Test," there are simply too many variables in the total complex called "teacher effectiveness." It suggested that research should be directed at strengthening the weakest point of an argument, namely, the variables among the lectures themselves. In order to make research more reliable in the matter of teacher effectiveness, we need to define exactly what is meant by *effectiveness* in teaching. It was suggested that more than one kind of effectiveness might be in operation. If we could

keep the ability level of the pupils constant, then the differences between classes will be due only to the teacher's teaching ability, and on
this point we need further proof of reliability.

One kind of reliability that further research might examine is,
How repeatable is the teachers performance? Do the same teachers
achieve the same results with different students? Perhaps there
should be a study on teacher-student interaction by systematically
matching types of students with types of teachers. In the previously
mentioned article, the question is raised, "Can a teacher who lectures well on volcanoes also lecture well on earthquakes or on the
meaning of art?" To illustrate the differences in teacher effectiveness,
seven student teachers took general science information from the *Scientific American* magazine and delivered short lectures. The tests administered following these lectures demonstrated considerable
differences in teacher effectiveness, since the student ability level,
teaching material, and teaching method were generally the same.[22]

It is true that many of the researchers were well aware of these
variables, which were difficult to control, and, in fact, admitted only
to the *probability* rather than the *proof* of their findings. Robert Thouless, in his introduction to McLeish's experiments, testified to this
weakness inherent in experimentation. "In the present monograph,
Dr. McLeish gives an account of research work carried out to find
answers to some of these questions. The answers given are obviously
still incomplete and tentative; unfortunately, research rarely provides the definitive answers demanded by the lovers of controversy.
No one can claim that research has established that lecturing is a
useless activity."[23] Despite this admission, however, Thouless ridi-
cules those educationalists who are hesitant to accept the findings of
such research. "The principle that educational procedures should be
guided by the results of research is not accepted as generally as one
might hope. In educational circles there is still often to be found a
preference for the excitements of verbal argumentation rather than
for the more prosaic activity of assessing the results of experiments.
It is to be hoped that this monograph series will help it to pass more
quickly!"[24]

Mollet, at the end of his study left a footnote indicating that the
conclusions of his study were not foolproof. "The present study does
not in any way indicate to what extent the response of the forty-six

students was representative of the students studying philosophy of education. Limitations of space exclude further enquiries in this paper."[25] Not only does he question the matter of not extending his study to include a greater number which would make the results more representative, but he wondered whether those students who did fill out and return the questionnaire were representative of the rest who decided not to answer his questions. "It would have been of interest, however, to see if there was any correlation, say between the students who have attained high marks during their stay at college and those students who returned the questionnaire."[26]

Even Donald Bligh, after all of his painstaking categorizations of the multitude of experiments of other researchers and those he himself conducted, conceded difficulty in arriving at truly scientific evidence in these experiments because of these variables. In his book *What's the Use of Lectures* under the caption "Reservations" he confessed: "Such arguments are never as tight as one wishes them to be. This is partly because of the inadequacy of scientific evidence in an area containing many interacting variables. This variety also makes such experiments very difficult to control." He added this consolation, "as in other professions teachers often have to take action on limited evidence, and within those limits I think the arguments are reasonable.[27]

The problem with these reservations and admissions becomes more acute because of the fact that these concessions usually appear in more or less inconspicuous places and not directly together with the conclusions. Furthermore, as a result (and probably because people will believe what they wish to believe), other researchers or laity will base their premises or beliefs on the result of these *difficult-to-control* experiments. It appears as though one of the researchers cited earlier has done precisely this, and has gone, perhaps, one step further in actually discouraging his readers from investigating any further for additional evidence. In the midst of an elucidation of the results of his experiment, Mollet made the following categorical statement. "Both McLeish and Bligh accept however, that the lecture system is not an efficient method for other objectives,"[28] (other than the transmission of a body of knowledge). Now with an air of infallibility Mollet comes forth with a sweeping statement concerning the experiments of McLeish and Bligh, which admittedly were difficult to control and not *tight* enough to make as good an argument as wished. "There would appear to be little point in seeking evidence to the contrary, for as Bligh states: 'I have not found a single study to suggest that lectures stimulate thought better than discussion methods.' "[29]

In connection with his Norwich Experiment, McLeish alluded to one of the criticisms of research in the use of experimental and control groups to determine effectiveness of the lecture — "seeking uniformity of delivery which is one of the variables cited above as difficult to standardize."[30] Even worse than this, however, in an effort to compensate for a lack of uniformity of delivery he resorted to another method of delivery, which further complicates the validity of these experiments, by using tape recordings of the lectures. He was quick to see the disadvantages, even though he felt he had solved the problem of uniformity of delivery. "The lecture has been given in the form of a tape-recording. This, of course, cuts out the visual impact, making it difficult to employ ancillary aids, such as blackboards, film projectors, effectively — without mentioning the facial grimaces, bodily contortions and extreme motor activity which some popular exponents of the lecture find invaluable in holding the attention of their audiences. This is one of the main barriers to generalising. . . ."[31]

Why would students (including grammar school youngsters who volunteered for this experiment) care to listen to a voice emanating from the loud speaker of a tape recorder, especially since it was on a subject of which they had no previous knowledge, and for which they had no particular interest? It would be just as sensible and fair to judge the impact of a television program by turning off the video and being exposed only to the audio stimulus. McLeish was correct in stating that in his attempts to keep the delivery consistent he had destroyed any nonverbal communication between speaker and listener. He failed, however, to concede that this procedure also cut out all possible feedback.

We can hardly equate this sort of experiment with what actually takes place in the real classroom. Furthermore, a number of these experiments were carried out in single or duplicate instances, and one should not arrive at any "scientific" conclusion from such a limited project. In reading about these experiments and the conclusions reached, how can one know whether or not a very lively face-to-face discussion group involving active student participation was being compared to a dull tape-recorded lecture? Why do more of these *scientific* studies not evaluate a truly interesting professionally trained lecturer and compare this performance and its results with those of other equally correct performances of another type of teaching technique?

Few Examples of Good Lecturers

We do not have to go very far in our search for the answers to the question raised here. The first reason is that too often it is difficult to locate such a well-trained or dynamic lecturer, due to a woeful lack of teacher training in communication arts.

Robert Thouless almost unashamedly rationalized the situation of poor lecturers in general when he wrote: "It may be said that the main defect of the lecture system is that there is no guarantee that these purposes are achieved even by the generality of performers." He was commenting on Paulsen's three main purposes of lecturing in higher education: "To provide a survey of a whole field of knowledge through the medium of a living personality; to relate this body of knowledge to the primary aims of human life; and to arouse an active interest, leading to an independent comprehension of the subject on the part of the listener."

Thouless continues, "If we take these declared objectives seriously as justification of the lecture, it can be asserted with confidence that the number of teachers capable of getting even some way towards achieving them at the established lecture hour every day for a considerable period of time must be decidedly small."[32] He is implying that even if we could find interesting lecturers, we could not expect them to keep up this splendid rhetorical excellence day after day. The following triple observation, quite consistent with logic, is even more astonishing. "If we take Paulsen's declaration as a serious statement of intent, and not mere rhetoric, it surely implies that lecturing is an *art* which requires special study and training; that probably few people are really capable of lecturing at all; and that no one would attempt to use the method over any length of time as an all-purpose vehicle." Having laid down the basic major and minor premise, Thouless now reached the inevitable conclusion to his implied disjunctive syllogism, namely, that we either find a different method for our untrained teachers, or we are responsible for producing mediocre lecturers in higher education.[33]

Why did he and other researchers and educators not switch this train of logical thoughts to an adjacent set of tracks and reason that since lecturing is an art, the effective performance of which too few are rightly trained, much greater emphasis should be laid upon a thorough background training in teaching methods and the communicative arts.

This line of reasoning seems the most logical. I am aware, however, that there are those like Bligh and Thouless who would immediately rise up to defend their positions in stating that what I am advocating is too idealistic in the first place, and, in the second place, even if lecturers were properly trained in the communicative arts their admirable performances would only meet with frustrations and would scarcely be worth all of the time and effort. Bligh wrote that improved effectiveness is often only temporary and insists that the *good* lecture is still nevertheless too weak to stand upon its own two feet and must be supported by another teaching method.

> There are innumerable experiments which show that improvements in presentation can lead to an increase in immediate learning, but that this advantage is lost in the ensuing week if no techniques are used to consolidate it. This is frustrating for teachers who strive to improve their teaching.[34]

Bligh, however, did not cite these "innumerable experiments" which indicate that the very best that a "professionally trained" lecturer can hope for in the use of the lecture method is only a temporary increase in learning.

It is little wonder that lectures and lecturers are often discredited and spoken of with disparagement. Instead of advocating that teachers prepare themselves for the many challenges to be encountered in lecturing, Thouless actually appeared intentionally to discourage the teacher who did attempt to lecture successfully, and, thereby endeavor to find a source of job satisfaction.

> If one is a university lecturer, the main competence on which one prides oneself may be skill in delivering a lecture in such a way that students are both interested and informed, and have their intellectual diffi-

culties resolved. To those whose "job-satisfaction" derives largely from their use of this skill, it is an uncomfortable thought that perhaps the skill may not be such a useful one as they had supposed, and that the university of the future may not include the activity of lecturing at all.[35]

PROFESSORS' SUSPICION TOWARD COMMUNICATION ARTS

Speech education is looked down upon by many professors and administrators as a "subacademic" discipline lacking in substantial content and dealing in "gadgetry and how-to-do-it methodology." In fact, most of the courses in the *practical* teaching area to be found in teaching methods are eyed with suspicion and perceived to be deficient in content significantly to be excluded from the curriculum. This suspicion of speech communication as a worthy academic discipline also stems from the fact that educators perceive coursework in such an art to be absent of consistent pattern or organization, and yet speech is one of the oldest disciplines, going back thousands of years to the days of the rhetoricians of Rome and Greece. There is also evidence that it was taught in ancient Egypt.

Proficiency in speaking is so often erroneously equated with polished oratory, acting and the dramatic. To some educators a *qualified* lecturer in their view would be, what today is considered an outdated elocutionist. Others feel that in order to be a good lecturer, one would have to possess the abilities and acquire the training background of an actor. In order to be a good lecturer, however, one does not have to become an orator, or comedian, as some would suggest. One simply needs to know and apply the rhetorical and psychological principles involved in public speaking and persuasion; in other words, one must be skilled in communicating concepts and enthusiasm to students. There are no genuine reasons why any teacher should shy away from improving performance because this skill has been used by the unscrupulous as a "manipulator of men's minds" or as artificial and insincere, or in some way suggestive of display, conceit, or even exploitation.

When McLeish feared criticism for employing tape recordings in his experiment, he spoke somewhat sarcastically (and inaccurately) in depicting the assumed artificiality of the public speaker's nonverbal cues, when referring to the "facial grimaces, bodily contortions and extreme motor activity which some popular exponents of the lecture find invaluable in holding the attention of their audiences."[36] I would suspect that he was here merely giving vent to his prejudices and mistrust of the arts, rather than describing actual beliefs and practices of "exponents of the lecture."

No doubt Eble tried to clarify this gross misconception of the lecture when he wrote the following:

> Teachers need to recognize the basic attractiveness of the lecture before they attempt to attack or defend it. University lecturing of the commonest kind is not the meticulously composed public address, nor is it even the speech that demands extensive advance preparation or the use of visual aids and demonstrations. No, it is the bare lecture, what a skilled teacher carries to class inside his skull with nothing for support but a book or two under his arm and notes in his hand. Delivered by a professor with a high degree of competence, classroom lectures may well achieve the objectives peculiar to their substance and impact: conveying information to a large audience with some expectation that this information is being received, and stimulating students to pursue specific or related learning on their own.[37]

PERSONAL INADEQUACIES IN LECTURING

Another reason we do not see more "good" lecturers in the classroom may be due to the fact (as mentioned earlier) that teachers are afraid to devote much time to lecturing for fear of failure. To rationalize their personal inadequacies they exaggerate and distort the disadvantages of lecturing, and by convincing themselves and others of the ineffectiveness of the lecture method they persuade themselves to resort to another teaching method and thus avoid the anxiety often associated with delivering a speech in public. Perhaps there may also be hidden feelings of jealousy by those who cannot, toward those who can, perform well in public. At times these feelings of inadequacies or misunderstandings are expressed in caricaturing and ridiculing of various aspects of the art of public speaking.

LECTURING DEMANDS HARD WORK

Yet another reason we see such a dearth of inspiring lecturers could be because it does take a lot of preparation and hard work along with certain native talents and acquired skills to do a consistently good job of lecturing. The effectiveness of the lecture correlates to a great extent with the level of talent, training, personal characteristics, and willpower, and in the way these are mobilized to achieve the objectives of teaching in a specific discipline.

In the preface of his book, Bligh compared lecturing to an art like musical composition and performance. He stated that skill in an art is acquired by practice rather than reading books. He failed in this excellent analogy, however, to point out that this practicing must *precede* the public performance. He borrowed another metaphor from Nisbet that lecturing is analogous to becoming proficient in driving a car. Nisbet suggested three levels of proficiency — the provisional driving license or permit during which time one learns the rules; the ordinary user in perfecting the everyday skills and the rally driver, whose personal styles override the conventional rules and driving habits. There was no mention of the fact that the *learner* practices his driving under the supervision of an experienced licensed driver and must pass a driving examination in which he must demonstrate not only his knowlege about driving, but also his ability in driving *before* receiving a license to drive a vehicle on public roads. Likewise the college and university professor should have received adequate theory and practice in teaching skills under competent supervision *prior* to the public performances in the classroom.

Thouless asked the question, "Is the lecture, *as commonly delivered* an effective way of conveying the kind of information required at university level?" If he was referring to the style of the very formal lecture, poorly read from a manuscript without flexibility in the unlikely event of feedback from the students, then it is not necessary for us to look at the testimonials of the educators, or listen to student protest or wade though the great mass of published research and funded studies in answering this question with an emphatic "no." It is a wonder that there exists any amount of competency in classroom lecturing. McLeish in his observation stated:

> Lacking the basic training in the arts of oratory and rhetoric and under present-day conditions of the restricted availability of the best models in theatre and lecture-room for imitation, it is indeed surprising that the average untrained university and other lecturer is capable of

performing at the level we find today in institutions of higher learning.[38]

IN DEFENSE OF LECTURING

Contrary to common belief, the lecture does not have to be a dull and uninteresting presentation of impersonal, irrelevant, factual information, but rather this teaching method can be inspiring and motivating and is capable of stimulating active student participation. It can be effectively and creatively employed in problem-centered situations and in development of understanding, as well as for the transfer of knowledge. Laing classified lectures as either didactic, inspirational or both didactic and inspirational.

> Some lectures, e.g. in literature, philosophy and fine arts, are designed to generate or increase enthusiasm for a subject, provoke thinking or guide taste. The communication of knowledge is a secondary aim. . . . A good didactic lecture can also be inspirational; the lecturer can so present the facts and conceptual structures of his subject and the methods of tackling it that he ensures not only that the student understands it but also that he develops an enthusiasm for it and is stimulated to pursue its study on his own.[39]

Frederick Mayer pleaded for the survival of lectureship and expressed the vast potentials of the lecture, which far surpasses the ordinary circumscribed place allotted to it in general.

> As long as faculties contain gifted lecturers, we must not think of the lecture as being obsolete, a survival of the medieval tradition. A great lecture is as significant as a brilliant symphony. When it touches the hearts and the imagination of students it has a lasting value. A lecture can be as problem-centered as a discussion: it can create a real sense of existential involvement between teacher and student.
>
> Unhappily, too many who lecture are not gifted that way. A deadly sin of a lecturer is to read from a book or use notes in a mechanical way. What the student wants is personal interpretation. General ideas remain vague and distant if they are not individualized. An inspired lecturer gives color to experience; he heightens the sensations of the moment. Students thus experience what Aristotle calls a catharsis, a projection of individuality into a universal realm.[40]

The lecture method is not restricted to the use of the most formal type of lecturing. The teacher can resort to a much less formal approach, incorporating question-and-answer periods, or use a combination of the lecture and discussion method. These variations will be more fully elaborated on in the chapters on attention and feedback.

WEAKNESSES OF OTHER TEACHING METHODS

Some of the same criticisms hurled against the lecture also are applicable to other methods of teaching. There are likewise many areas where the teacher can fail to communicate effectively in the use of other techniques.

Discussion Method

In my twenty-three years of college teaching in the area of discussion techniques and communication skills, I have been able to observe some common weaknesses and limitations in the discussion method. In general, the average instructor has had no more training in leading out in a discussion, which can in itself present a real problem and become difficult to handle, or the instructor, acting as chairperson, because of lack of training or preparation might ramble on more or less aimlessly and end up doing most of the talking himself as in the so-called *monologue* of the lecture. There is absolutely nothing as dull and uninteresting as a discussion on a topic of comparatively little initial interest, inadequate student and teacher preparation, and poor leadership. On the other hand, however, with the right kind of a subject and initial interest, alert students who have spent considerable time researching the topic, together with proper leadership of an experienced instructor, can provide lively and educationally profitable discussions.

Feedback and active participation of the majority of students in a discussion group can be just as lacking as in poor lecturing. Needless to say, it is very difficult, if not impossible, for much student participation to take place in large classes, which often number into the hundreds. Any teaching situation involving more than two dozen or possibly a total of thirty students, spontaneous, free discussion becomes either inhibited or entered into only by a small percentage of the students. In every class there seems to be one individual (or two) who thinks he knows it all, plainly "inebriated with his own verbosity" and monopolizes the discussion, and it repeatedly becomes necessary for the instructor to endeavor to stop such students and encourage others to participate. Other students, because of their shyness, hesitancy, or other reasons, simply never contribute to the discussion.

The discussion method is not always effective in the presentation of factual material, value judgment, or problem solving. After all, the professor has spent years in acquiring information and knowledge and must schedule the material that must be covered in a given course. Even with a lively discussion this method can be very time-consuming. In ordinary situations, it would be wishful thinking to hope for effective, productive discussions to be forthcoming every week or several times a week throughout the entire course. Even though there are advantages in the discussion method, such as student participation and the pooling of knowledge, as well as learning to cooperate or in being more tolerant of other people's viewpoints, it can end up being a waste of class time with no real decisions made or even concluding with the wrong answers. Instead of discussion becoming a "pooling of knowledge and information," it can, without proper leadership, degenerate into a "pooling of ignorance and misinformation." The report of the Committee on Undergraduate Teaching expressed these failings succinctly:

> Many professors have difficulty in establishing their roles as discussion leaders because they have never had opportunity to participate in an expertly handled discussion, and so have no model ready at hand. In consequence, they tend to commit common errors that reduce the usefulness of discussion. Pace learned, for example, from university and liberal arts college students alike that lively discussions were rare in their experience. . . . There is good evidence that it can be a powerful means for inducing thoughtfulness about problems to which neither the teacher nor anyone else have satisfactory answers. It can, that is, if the teacher, employing the Socratic approach, involves the students in the common task of exploration.[41]

The Seminar

The seminar, in which smaller groups of students assemble to present papers and then discuss the material, is also subject to some of the same pitfalls as the discussion or lecture. If carried on successfully the teacher must carefully prepare the students by laying a good groundwork for the student's research and in motivating each researcher to insure that the presentation of papers will be worthwhile and meaningful. It is necessary for the teacher to spend a considerable amount of time in guiding each student in the writing of his papers, and in directing the seminar evaluations and discussions, otherwise a lot of time and energy will be exerted largely in vain, because of inferior scholarship. The seminar, obviously, is definitely limited to a small number of students.

The Tutorials

Tutorials can result in effective learning as the professor gives still more personal help to an individual student or several students in directive studies or research projects. In this teaching method, the instructor can discover in what particular areas of a discipline the student is lacking and give special help in these areas. Only a very limited number of students can thus be assisted each year. Furthermore, there is always the fear on both the part of the teacher and the part of the student that in this one-to-one teaching and learning situation, one or the other (or both) might be horribly dull and uninteresting, or that a proper relationship cannot be forthcoming, creating a clash of personalities, or complete apathy.

Closely related to the tutorials is the directed or independent study. Even though this type of a learning program has some definite advantages for some, it often needs the guidance of an experienced teacher, and certainly the motivation and initiative of an ambitious or at least more mature student.

In each individual method or combination of teaching methods (and modifications of these techniques) there are potential barriers to communication. As Eble expressed it, "Mediocre discussion classes, poor individual student reports, ineffectual panel presentations are no improvement upon a teacher's mediocre lecturing."[42]

Each college and university teacher must be fully aware of the communication pitfalls in each of the teaching methods and must carefully evaluate which method or combination of techniques would be most suited to the nature of the subject, interest and maturity of the students, to his own personality and "enlightened" ability in fulfilling the objectives and the course of the general aims of higher education.

NOTES

1. Powell, Len: *Lecturing*. London, Pitman Pub., 1973, p. 4.
2. Powell, Len: *Lecturing*. p. 4.
3. Rovin, Sheldon, Lalonde, Ernest, and Haley, John H.: An assessment of the Lecture. *Improving College and University Teaching, 20*:326, Autumn, 1972.
4. Editorial: A talking teacher cannot succeed. *Improving College and University Teaching, 7*:67, 1959.
5. Glicksberg, Charles I.: Is lecturing teaching? *Improving College and University Teaching, 6*:27, 28, 1958.
6. Editorial: A talking teacher cannot succeed, *7*:67, 1959.
7. Glicksberg, Charles I.: Is lecturing teaching? *6*, 27.
8. Bligh, Donald, Ebrahim, G.J., Jaques, David, and Piper, D. Warren: *Teaching Students*. Devon, England, Exeter University Teaching Services, a EUTS Production, 1975, p. 103.
9. Editorial: A student forum. *Improving College and University Teaching, 17*:163, 1969 (quoting Tyson, Stephen E.).
10. Glicksberg, Charles: Is lecturing teaching? p. 27.
11. Mollet, David: Students' evaluation of teaching methods and changes in teaching methods, *Assessment in Higher Education, 2*, No. *2*:136-149, February, 1977.
12. Bligh, Donald, et. al.: *Teaching Students*. p. 105.
13. McLeish, John: *The Lecture Method*. Cambridge, Cambridge Institute of Education, 1968, Introduction, pp. vii, viii, quoting Robert H. Thouless.
14. McLeish, John: *The Lecture Method*. pp. 4-12.
15. McLeish, John: *The Lecture Method*. pp. 5, 6.
16. McLeish, John: *The Lecture Method*. p. 6.
17. Bligh, Donald A.: *What's the Use of Lectures?* Exeter, D.A. and B. Bligh, 1971, pp. 5-25.
18. Bligh, Donald A.: *What's the Use of Lectures?* pp. 4, 23, 25.
19. Bligh, Donald et. al.: *Teaching Students*. pp. 101-103.
20. Sandford, N. (Ed.): *The American College*. McKeachie, W.J.: Procedures and techniques of teaching: a survey of experimental studies. New York, Wiley,

1962, p. 325.

21. Bligh, Donald et. al.: *Teaching Students.* p. 105.
22. Rudin, Stanley A.: Measuring the teacher's effectiveness as a lecturer. *Journal of Genetic Psychology, 98*:153, 154, 1961.
23. McLeish, John: *The Lecture Method.* p. viii.
24. McLeish, John: *The Lecture Method.* p. viii.
25. Mollet, David: Students' evaluation of teaching methods and changes in teaching methods. p. 155.
26. Mollet, David: Students' evaluation of teaching methods and changes in teaching methods, p. 155.
27. Bligh, Donald A.: *What's the Use of Lectures?* p. 25.
28. Mollet, David: Students' evaluation of teaching methods and changes in teaching methods. p. 155.
29. Mollet, Students' evaluation, p. 155
30. McLeish, John: *The Lecture Method.* p. 5.
31. McLeish, John: *The Lecture Method.* p. 5.
32. McLeish, *The Lecture Method,* p. 2
33. McLeish, John: *The Lecture Method.* p. 2.
34. Bligh, Donald A. et. al.: *Teaching Students.* p. 103.
35. McLeish, John: *The Lecture Method.* p. vii.
36. McLeish, John: *The Lecture Method.* p. 5.
37. Eble, Kenneth E.: *The Craft of Teaching.* San Francisco, Jossey-Bass Pub., 1976, p. 43.
38. McLeish, John: *The Lecture Method.* p. 2.
39. Laing, A.: the art of lecturing. In Layton, David (Ed.): *University Teaching in Transition.* Edinburgh, Oliver and Boyd, Ltd., 1968, pp. 18, 19.
40. Mayer, Frederick: Creative teaching, *Improving College and University Teaching, 8, No. 1*:42, Winter, 1960.
41. Rothwell, C. Easton, Chairman: *The Importance of Teaching.* New Haven, Connecticut, The Hazen Foundation, 1968, p. 47, quoting C.R. Pace.
42. Eble, Kenneth E.: *The Craft of Teaching.* pp. 42, 43.

CHAPTER 5

PLANNING AND ORGANIZING THE LECTURE

The good lecturer not only teaches his subject-matter logically and well but actively assists his students to sort out and arrange the various items of learning in order of priority and significance. This ensures a sense of structure while infusing meaning into the presentation.

Henderson

Don't come to your lecture with a potpourri of ill-digested materials hastily put together the night before or of material mugged up from textbooks which you know the students themselves are unlikely to possess.

Laing

EVEN though a teacher may be an expert in the subject area, have an acceptable personality, and be dedicated to the work of teaching, communication in the classroom can break down if there is a lack of planning and organization. The importance of adequate preparation for, and proper organization of a course, as well as of each individual class session can not be overemphasized. This is particularly true of the lecture course and each lecture.

Unless each one in the class, from the very beginning of the term, knows the aims and objectives, the student will not have a clear idea just where he is going and what will be expected each day and throughout the entire course. The relationship of the course to the departmental and institutional aims and objectives and the purpose of higher education itself should be clarified and carefully delineated.

It has been said that one of the best ways of learning a subject thoroughly is by having to lecture on that subject. Clarity of exposition is not possible, however, unless it is first clearly understood by the instructor. Moreover, thorough knowledge of the subject matter insures that the teacher can devote most of the mental energies to organizing the material in such a way that the listeners will not only understand it but will also be stimulated to give further study to it.

Without a definite goal or destination clearly in mind, and without sufficient signposts along the way, it is very difficult for the students to relate to what is being presented. They lose all sense of direction and purpose; consequently, vital teacher-student communication breaks down. Let us suppose that we are about to board a jumbo jet. What would be our reaction if, upon asking the pilot where the plane was going, he replied that he did not actually have any definite destination in mind? If we were about to embark on a long voyage and discovered that the captain of the ship had no particular port in mind, we would be confused (and frightened). Many a course of study has gotten off course and has been shipwrecked (or crashed) because of lack of purpose and organization.

On the first day or two of the course, it is essential to clearly present (orally and in written form) the aims and objectives of the course and the materials to be used, such as textbook, additional reading, etc. The teaching methods or techniques should be explained and hints given as to how the students will be evaluated through tests, essays, reports, etc. The outline or syllabus, distributed at this time can be very detailed and complete or need not be so specific as to describe what is to be covered each day of the course. It should provide a broad format, allowing for flexible presentation within each week or time unit in the progression of the course.

The preparation and organization of the first several class sessions are extremely important, because it is at this time the teacher not only gives direction and meaning to the entire course but also motivates the students by portraying what they will have learned and be able to do at the end of the course, thereby encouraging each one to put forth his best efforts. As mentioned in the chapter on personality, this is also the most decisive time of the entire course in which the important teacher-student relationship and the general classroom atmostphere are set. All further communication will suffer if the teacher fails to lay a solid groundwork for successful communication during the remainder of the course. Careful preparation and logical organization of these introductory lectures may require a considerable amount of time and much thought, but the teacher will be well rewarded in thus commencing an effective learning process.

What has been said about clearly defining the purpose and objectives of the course as a whole can also be applied to each lecture or class session. The topic, theme or problem under consideration for that day's lecture and discussion should be established at the start of each class period. Each lecture ought to be a separate complete unit, but a brief review of previous material covered might be very helpful so that each unit of instruction can be related to what has been presented, and to the overall course material. In most of the teacher evaluations, students rank clarity and organization high on the list of the qualifications of an effective teacher. By this they do not necessarily mean that everything the instructor says must be categorized and classified into a meticulously organized pattern or laboriously explained, but they become confused, as well as bored, when the teacher just rambles on. Organization is most valued when it simplifies, clarifies and shows relationship to a meaningful purpose and relevancy to life situations, and not simply shows design for the sake of symmetry. In the area of organization, as in other aspects of public speaking and communicative skills, teacher education and training are woefully lacking in the undergraduate and graduate studies. Many courses are required to enable the future teacher to be knowledgeable in the field of specialization, but these courses seldom prepare the teacher with the knowledge and ability to organize this material for effective presentation.

PURPOSE AND TYPES OF OUTLINES

The effective teacher must not only recognize the *importance* of preparing the material day by day for classroom presentation in an organized fashion, but must know *how* to gather and outline this material. I would like to enumerate five purposes (or benefits) that will be derived from organizing lecture material into an outline form, and then briefly describe several different *types* of outlines that can be appropriately used in varying circumstances.

When the teacher has a definite purpose or objective in mind and has selected a particular topic through which he can develop his ideas toward the intended goal, he must carefully order these thoughts in some kind of logical sequence. Only then will the lecture have a sense of direction and clarity of expression. For the following five reasons it is imperative for the teacher to have a well-ordered outline.

1. Initially, the rough outline will greatly assist in *gathering* information and ideas for class presentation. As material can be located on various aspects of the subject under consideration, it can immediately be classified or categorized in one of the broad areas of the division in the rough outline. One idea will lead to another related one, and soon everything falls into line.

2. As the various aspects of the outline develop and the outline nears completion, the teacher can begin to judge the amount of information that can be used in the alloted time. Thus, the outline will be useful in *timing* the material for a given lecture period, thereby indicating whether there will be sufficient or too much material to present in the class time. The outline serves as a guide in preparation for delivery.

3. The outline will enable the teacher to *deliver* the thoughts in a logical and meaningful way. By having the general sequence of ideas of the outline well in mind, the instructor can then proceed with the unfolding or the development of the thoughts easily within minimum dependence on notes or script. In using an outline from which to deliver the lecture, the professor will not be tempted to read the lecture, nor slavishly adhere to notes as with the use of a verbatim manuscript. The outline, however, will help prevent the lecturer from wandering from the intended ideas or from being unduly distracted, and yet, at the same time, will allow for flexibility in adding fresh, relevant thoughts which may flash into the teacher's mind as the

feedback is read and interpreted in a truly communicative event.

Perhaps the reason why so many teachers feel they must write out their lectures word for word is not necessarily because their memory is so poor, but because their ideas are so poorly related to one another that it is impossible to remember them. The matter of whether a lecture should be read from a script or delivered extemporaneously will be discussed in the chapter dealing with attention and interest.

4. The use of an outline not only benefits the teacher in the matter of gathering, organizing, timing, and delivering the lecture, but it also becomes a *positive aid to the listener* in making the lecture both interesting and meaningful. The student knows where he is going, and as the ideas progress and develop from point to point, the listener feels involved in the lecture as it moves along, not too rapidly, or dragging along too slowly, but unfolding section by section until the entire concept or fact clearly stands out in his own mind.

If the lecture is well-organized and delivered properly, the student can follow what is being said without weariness of mind, which results from an attempt at rearranging the ideas into some kind of meaningful whole.

5. Finally, the lecture delivered correctly from a clear outline will be *retained* in the mind of the student much longer, because the main points, as well as many of the subordinate subpoints have stood out in his memory. We are told that almost immediately there is almost a 50 percent loss of retention in any oral communication. This fact emphasizes the need and importance for every teacher to present lectures which are clearly ordered. A lack of organization is a major communication breakdown in the learning process.

TYPES OF OUTLINES

Several different types of outlines can be used in lecturing. First of all, let us consider outlining those which deal primarily with the transfer of factual information. At the very beginning of the class period before the presention of any new material, it is beneficial to review briefly the main points of the last lecture and then introduce the various broad categories that are to be discussed in the current lecture, emphasizing relationship and continuity. A relatively simply and most generally used outline in organizing information is the development of logical grouping or classification. Every subject lends itself to some sort of natural divisions. No topic should ever be *forced* to fit an artificially constructed outline. The subject should be divided into natural segments. First of all, the main divisions should be kept few in number, and also the subdivisions should not exceed three or four. Only one general area should be dealt with at a time, and all of the material relating to a specific aspect of the subject should be grouped together and thoroughly explained before proceeding on to the next item. All new terms should be elucidated by definition, by examples and possibly at times by appropriate visual aids and even demonstrations.

Before going on to the next major division of the topic, a brief summary, recapitulation or restatement is helpful to clinch a point in the minds of the students before introducing another area of the subject. This is also an excellent time for the instructor to invite any questions on the material thus far covered. This internal summary should be followed by a transitional phrase or sentence such as, "Now let us consider another type (or quality, purpose, benefit, etc.) of. . . ." Like a caption within a chapter, these transitions indicate to the students that one section of the topic has now been covered and attention is about to be drawn to another phase of the subject.

Another type of lecture material that lends itself well, and with minimum effort, to organization and outlining is that which involves a problem for which solutions are sought. In the introductory remarks, the lecturer may capture the attention of the students and involve them in the subject by beginning with a startling statement of fact or opinion, a rhetorical question or series or rhetorical questions or a graphic real or hypothetical illustration. (More of this will be noted in the chapter on interest and attention.) During the introduction the students must realize the importance of the problem and be aware of its significance to society and to themselves so that from the very start of the lecture they will decide to listen carefully and become personally involved.

Usually such a presentation will begin with the first major division, a declaration of the problem itself, and a definition of terms as well as a limitation or narrowing of the problem to specific segments of the overall situation. What are the facts about the problem? How extensive is it? What effects can be seen, or what potential dangers and consequences might be expected? Actually, these three questions could very well constitute three subdivisions of the first major point, which can be the assertion and acknowledgment of the problem.

After nailing down exactly what the problem is and making certain that everyone is aware of its significance, a transitional statement or question leads right into the next major division. "Why do you think this problem exists to such an extent in our country (or in other countries of the world)? For example, let us say that the lecture is on juvenile delinquency (obviously too broad for a single lecture). After discussing the seriousness of the problem and how it is everyone's concern, the lecturer is ready to deal with the *causes* of the problem. The members of the class can be asked to help enumerate the various causes, and out of this jumble of diverse causes, the teacher should classify them into distinct areas, such as those which relate to the *home*, the *school* environment, and the *community*, and then elaborate on the ways in which each area contributes to the total problem. The student can now remember three general groupings, whereas it would have been very difficult, if not impossible, to have remembered fifteen or more causes suggested in random fashion by the students. Practically all of these suggested causes now fit neatly into the above three categories.

What is there in the home that could be a cause of juvenile delinquency? The answer, at least in part, can be traced to the parents. Here is an excellent opportunity for the lecturer to write the main divisions and subpoints on the blackboard as each one is being discussed. What is there about the parents in the home that could cause children to go wrong? Immediately the answers will fall into line — as the teacher (and students) list these possible causes — drinking, constant quarreling and strife, insecurity and divorce, parents being too lenient or too strict, inadequate love or overprotection, etc. Going on to the next subdivision of causes in the home, what else beside parents in the home could bring about attitudes that eventually lead to a life of crime? It could be the position of the child in relationship to other children in the family or doting grandparents or other relatives. Uncontrolled television viewing by all the younger members of the family has been demonstrated to have an effect upon the attitude of children toward the sacredness of life, marriage, and the home. The same development continues for the other aspects of causes, such as the school and the community.

During the unfolding of the first two major divisions of this lectures the problem and causes, it is hoped that the students have become personally involved in a sense of responsibility and feeling of urgency that something needs to be done about the situation. At this psychological (and logical) juncture in the lecture, the transition to the final division is both easy and natural as the instructor asks the class what *solutions* they could offer to the problem. Once again, out of the great variety of answers, the lecturer can set down possible solutions on the blackboard, and then classify them into the three general categories (paralleling those of the causes) for solutions in the home, school, and community. One of the purposes of higher education is to lead the student to think for himself, have an opinion and furthermore, to be able to defend that opinion. It is within the power of the professor to motivate the students to take action and become personally interested and involved in solving the problem.

The same general format can be used in practically all issues connected with a problem-centered subject, but day after day this type of an outline, as useful as it may be, could become too repetitious, and, therefore, diminish in its effectiveness. Monroe suggested five different *formats* in outlining according to various patterns of sequences:

1. *Chronological* or time sequence, most usable in teaching such subjects as history, or at least during those lectures dealing mainly with specific events in the past. This outline simply is a division of successive time periods.

2. *Spacial* or geographical sequence can be beneficial in comparing different areas of a county or countries in such aspects as the geographical, social, ethnical, linguistical or historical development. Each major area being compared simply constitutes a separate division in the outline. Take, for example, a lecture on the three principle American dialects; Eastern,

Southern, and General American. These three form a natural and easy ordering of the information. There are variations, of course, within these broad areas, and these would be classified as subpoints.

3. The *problem-solution* sequence used for problem-centered subjects.

4. *Cause-effect* sequence, which is closely related to the problem-solution format. Probably the most frequently used sequence is a combination of the last two, as applied to the example of the outline on juvenile delinquency, which consists of I. The Problem, which is essentially the same as *effect*; II. The Causes; and, III. The Solutions.

5. *Special Topical* sequence, can actually be used for most subjects, but lends itself best to information-type presentations. To illustrate this sequence, we need a topic which has nothing to do with the history of anything, or characteristics of any political or geographical location; nor does it deal with a problem. It simply relates to the logical and natural parts of the subject itself. In a lecture, for example, on Law Enforcement Officers, the special topical sequence could be used rather than the problem-solution outline. The first division might be "Qualifications," the second, "Training," and the third, "Duties of Law Enforcement Officers." Under the first point, it would be logical to categorize the many and varied qualifications in three or four groupings or subpoints, such as: A. Physical, B. Intellectual, C. Moral, and D. Emotional or Psychological. The outline would be something like the following sample (in brief rather than full-content form):

I. Qualifications of a person wishing to become an officer of the law.
   A. Physical
      1. Appearance
         a. No visible marks of identification — scars, etc.
         b. Well-groomed
      2. Height
      3. General health
   B. Intellectual
      1. I.Q.

    2. Education — degrees

    3. Aptitude

  C. Moral

  D. Psychological or Emotional Stability

II. Training of persons preparing for service as officers of the law.

  A. Education

    1. Courses in criminal law

    2. Special courses in government, etc.

  B. Training in defense

    1. Use of weapons

    2. Self defense — karate

III. Duties of officers (or types of service)

  A. Government

  B. Regional

  C. Local

  D. Plain clothes police

  E. Criminal Investigation

A few simple rules to follow in the mechanics of the outline are (1) Each division should be a single separate unit. (2) There should be parallel structure in all of the main points. (3) All subpoints should be properly subordinated. (4) A consistent set of symbols should be used.[1]

DEDUCTIVE AND INDUCTIVE ARRANGEMENTS

There are actually several ways of developing a problem-centered lecture. The lecturer has the option of going in one of two directions. One is the Aristotelian approach of *deductive* movement from the general truth to the particular application, while *inductive* is the reverse of this process. Deduction is the process by which generalizations are applied to particulars, whereas induction is the process by which relationships are discovered and then generalized. In the deductive method, so widely used for many centuries, the main points are cases that are first stated and then broken down into subpoints, and these are often divided into even finer subpoints. The generalizations are illustrated, explained, and then applied.

The great danger in using the deductive approach is that the professor, after lengthy research, arrives at a conclusion which then becomes the basis upon which the lecture is built. The main portion of the time is spent on establishing the evidence to substantiate the proposition or conclusions arrived at as a result of careful study. In other words, the lecture evolves in the opposite direction of the research, which began with particulars or specifics and ended with a general conclusion. Why should the professor invert or reverse this process? Why should the students not be led on the same inductive journey of discovery in examining the specific details and then together with their instructor arrive at a conclusion, either explicit or implied? In fact, the wise teacher will often create such an "inductive" environment, which will allow and indeed encourage the students to continue to think about and work out a conclusion of their own. A good teacher does not do the thinking *for* the student but thinks *with* the student. This is the reason why, perhaps, the best teachers often do not receive as much credit from their students because the students believe they are thinking for themselves and that the conclusions arrived at are really their own.

ORGANIZATION OF DISCUSSIONS

In the discussion method, it is just as important or even more important (than the lecture) for teacher and students to have a definite purpose and clear organization of material. As mentioned earlier, it is very easy for the discussion to get off the main track, to bog down, or simply stagnate. Before the students are assigned research for the forthcoming discussion, they must have a clear understanding of the definition of terms and subject limitiations or particular emphasis. Furthermore, each one must have a clear concept of the sequence of areas to be covered and the specific divisions of the subject in order to efficiently gather materials for contribution during the group discussion. The teacher, or whoever is assigned to be the chairperson or discussion leader, must then guide the discussion in accordance with the previously declared outline. If the discussion relates to a problem, the outline might be as follows:

    I. Definitions of terms and limitations of topic.

II. A history or the background of the problem, or causes creating the situation.

III. The present situation, or extent and intensity of the current problem.

IV. The suggested and attempted solutions (and reasons why they have not been completely successful).

V. The solutions which the class members feel will solve the problem.

This type of a discussion outline could serve such topics as prison reform, social service reform, tax reform, censorship in mass media, inflation, energy crisis, integration or discrimination (school, housing or employment), and most other problems for which satisfactory solutions are being sought.

As mentioned in the last chapter, the discussion method of teaching has the disadvantages of being very time-consuming, and the discussants do not always come to a concrete decision or there exists a diversity of opinions. It is often difficult to keep the discussion on the subject, and there are often spots when the discussion drags. To prevent these communication breakdowns in discussion, it is imperative that the one who leads the class adheres quite strictly to the given outline and keeps it moving along. As in the lecture, so in the discussion, before moving on to the next point in the outline, the leader must summarize the points brought forth in the current division of the outline and then lead into the following main division with a transitional phrase or sentence.

The outline for the discussion class period generally follows the inductive approach to teaching, because it begins with the particulars and leads to the general conclusion. The inductive principle will help to eliminate many of the criticisms of both the lecture and the discussion. It has the tendency of involving the students throughout the presentation of the subject so that, in the case of the discussion, it encourages more spontaneous response and participation, keeps it moving along, and arrives at more definite conclusions. In the case of the lecture the inductive approach diminishes the feeling of the presentation being a *monologue*, polarizing the teacher-student relationship. It does not leave the student passive and the professor authoritative. In the inductive method, there is a joint and cooperative endeavor or search by instructor and learner in an examination of the hypothesis leading to the formulation of a plausible theory.

K. Patricia Cross, in her paper, "The Instructional Revolution," predicted another student rebellion in the 1980s protesting against the quality of their learning experience but added that this dissatisfaction can be avoided by teaching innovations. She then alluded to the Keller Plan:

> We are beginning to apply what we know about the teaching-learning process to college teaching. One of the pioneers of the instructional revolution is Fred Keller, a psychologist who simply applied what he had been teaching about learning to the design of his own classes. The Keller Plan, which is also known as the Personalized System of Instruction or PSI, has spread rapidly throughout the social and physical sciences. The learning principles incorporated into PSI are simple: 1. the learning tasks must be clearly defined; 2. students must respond actively; 3. immediate rewards must be granted for appropriate responses; and 4. foundation units must be learned well before advanced units are attempted.[2]

The students in these classes rated the courses higher than the usual lecture course in the same subjects and seemed to retain their learning longer. There is, however, nothing new about these principles of teaching. They are just logical and consistent with the communication theories applied to the learning process. In this chapter we have discussed the first of the PSI principles, namely, that "the learning tasks must be clearly defined."[3] Other aspects of these principles will be dealt with in such chapters as interest, motivation, listening, and feedback.

Henderson set down some commonsense principles of lecturing to large classes:

a. Have a definite aim or purpose in each lecture.
b. Prepare your work carefully.
c. Present your subject-matter in a logical sequence, proceeding from the known to the unknown.
d. Demonstrate and illustrate wherever possible.
e. Stimulate interest by the use of teaching aids.
f. Test each principle taught before proceeding to the next — at least by rhetorical question, or inviting discussion.
g. Let students ask the questions.
h. Let the students take an active part in the discussion and give them something to do afterwards. Remember "we learn to do

by doing."

    i. Recapitulate frequently, and test the efficiency of your instruction at some stage. . . . Clinching or pulling together the main points at the end of a lecture establishes fuller meaning and a sense of unity in the students' minds.[4]

STUDENT EVALUATION OF ORGANIZATION

According to the Marris inquiry (1965) the students desired lectures to be "clear, orderly synopses, logically planned, emphasizing basic principles and with not too many digressions."[5]

In a study by Cooper and Foy (1967), students and staff in a university department of pharmacy were asked to list statements describing lecturers' characteristics in order of importance. The first ten included the following ones, which relate directly to our discussion of clear organization and thorough preparation:

1. presents the material clearly and logically.
2. enables the student to understand the basic principle of the subject. . . .
4. shows an expert knowledge of his subject.
5. adequately covers the ground in the lecture course.
6. maintains continuity in the course. . . .
8. makes his material intelligibly meaningful.[6]

A number of characteristics have been consistently identified as comprising effective teaching. Hildebrand and Wilson (1970) and Eble (1970) both listed as the first major factor in good instruction "clarity of organization, interpretation and explanation."[7]

J.R. Trott stated that it is an absolute necessity for the lecturer to plan carefully and to prepare thoroughly each lecture in order to be able to communicate most effectively in the classroom.

> Planning and preparation are an absolute prerequisite for a good lecture. This seems so fundamental that it is surprising how many men believe that because they have the knowledge, all they have to do is to fill in the necessary time burbling garrulously, but ineffectually before an undergraduate audience. A lecture must be prepared; preferably so perfectly prepared that the lecturer can pursue his train of reasoning from the beginning to the end, without any notes, and yet be logical, clear cut and get across the cardinal points he is trying to make. Most of us have

not reached this stage, but need notes or headings to keep us on the right track. This is perfectly justifiable, but to write a lecture out in longhand and read a prepared statement is unforgivable, except where one is delivering some highly difficult research problem to a very select audience of scientific minds.[8]

It may seem that this is highly idealistic and not at all realistic or probable. Some even consider it to be a high standard impossible of attaining. William R. Hutchinson in *Learning and the Professors* compared the time and energy necessary for the preparation and presentation of a lecture to that of a clergyman's sermon, and considered it almost impossible for the lecturer to become anything more than a mediocre performer because of the considerable number of lectures required each week.

> Even the omnicompetent and the inexhaustible are usually giving too many lectures per week to do their students much good. It is not uncommon for clergymen to feel that one twenty-minute sermon deserves two days' preparation. Academic lecturers working with less divine and no secretarial assistance, probably should not inflict fifty minutes of scholarly material upon their students without equivalent preparation. Teachers, like ministers may be forced to use old lectures without revising them. . . . Surely this is not something our system should encourage. The common practice, therefore, of requiring college teachers to give from six to fifteen public lectures per week is a way of insisting upon mediocre performance.[9]

Hutchinson felt that even revising old notes could easily take one day for each lecture. Without proper undergraduate and graduate training this would, indeed, be a most difficult undertaking. However, with adequate training in teaching methods and communicative skills plus dedication, this is not an impossible, unrealistic, or unreasonable expectation of the college and university professor.

So important is this matter of thorough class preparation that it becomes one of the distinguishing characteristics of effective teaching, as Edward Sheffield has pointed out. "The chosen professors put great stress on thorough preparation for class sessions. Indeed, this may be one of the practices by which effective teachers are most easily distinguished from ineffective ones. They are dedicated, conscientious, and demanding both of themselves and their students. They work hard at teaching."[10]

There is little doubt that one of the major barriers to effective classroom communication is a lack of purpose and organization structure in which there is no systematic arrangement of ideas, materials, and words into any obvious and coherent order or without purpose, meaning and central idea. Clear organization is the mark of a clear message.

NOTES

1. Monroe, Alan H., and Ehninger, Douglas: *Principles and Types of Speech,* 6th ed. Glenview, Scott, Foresman and Co., 1967, Chapters 14 and 18.
2. Cross, K. Patricia: *The Instructional Revolution.* Paper presented at Concurrent General Session I, 31st National Conference of Higher Education, March 8, 1976, p. 5.
3. Cross, K. Patricia: *The Instructional Revolution.* p. 5.
4. Henderson, Norman K.: *University Teaching.* Hong Kong, Hong Kong University Press, 1969, pp. 17-19.
5. Beard, Ruth M., Bligh, D. A., and Harding, A.G.: *Research into Teaching Methods in Higher Education,* 4th ed. Guildford, Surrey, Society for Research into Higher Education, April, 1978, p. 35.
6. Beard, Ruth M. et. al.: *Research into Teaching Methods in Higher Education.* p. 42.
7. Trent, James W., and Cohen, Arthur M.: Research on teaching in higher education. In Travers, Robert M.W. (Ed.): *Second Handbook of Research on Teaching.* Chicago, Rand McNally and Co., 1973, p. 1044.
8. Trott, J.R.: Lectures, lecturers, and the lectured. *Improving College and University Teaching, 11, No. 2*:73, Spring, 1963.
9. Milton, Ohmer, and Shoben, Edward Joseph (Eds.): *Learning and the Professors.* Athens, Ohio University Press, 1968, p. 43, quoting Hutchinson, William R.: *Improving College and University Teaching, 17*:107, 1969.
10. Sheffield, Edward R. (Ed.): *Teaching in the Universities: No One Way.* Montreal, McGill-Queen's University Press, 1974, p. 205.

CHAPTER 6

INTEREST AND ATTENTION
IN THE CLASSROOM

The responsibility of inattentiveness is squarely on the speaker. There is no such thing as an inattentive audience. What the speaker really would have meant was the audience was not attending to him. In such a case, his speech must have been boring, trite, unclear, disorganized, lacking in vital materials, indirect or unanimated. So the audience attended to something else.

Brembeck and Howell

ALTHOUGH in previous chapters it has already been implied that a lack of interest and attention often characterized the lecture method and can also plague the discussion, seminar, and tutorial techniques as well, this particular barrier to classroom communication will be dealt with specifically in this chapter.

It is almost superfluous to say that without interest there will be little attention, and without attention communication will not and, indeed, cannot take place. To the degree and intensity of interest and attention, communication is effective or ineffective. It is safe to say then that a lack of interest and attention constitute major causes for partial or complete breakdown of communication in teaching and learning processes in the college and university classroom.

If it were possible for a teacher to be guilty of all of the other communication barriers already mentioned in the previous chapters and also lacking in all of the areas to be covered in the following chapters, but at the same time, if the classroom lecturer would have this one single virtue of being interesting, there would still be some communication in the teacher-student relationship. On the other hand, however, it actually would not be possible to be competent in any of the other areas covered in this book, and yet totally, or even to a great extent, be lacking in interest and attention.

It is of such vital importance for the instructor to create an interest and to capture the attention of the students that this facet of the learning process permeates and pervades every other aspect of learning (and teaching), and, indeed, becomes a central focal point in the entire educational process. Some of the causes for a lack of interest and attention to be considered in this chapter have been alluded to in the last four chapters, and it would be very difficult to be silent in the following chapters relative to this communication breakdown in teaching. I have, therefore, placed this chapter in a central position among the other chapter topics, and am giving it a centric point in the entire communication concept.

First of all, I wish to analyze and explain the psychological as well as the physiological features of this problem briefly. Second, I will relate these principles to the conditions of classroom boredom and apathy and enumerate some of the causes for a lack of interest and attention, and finally, I will explore a number of ways in which this deadly barrier to communication can be reduced or removed.

NATURE OF ATTENTION

O'Neill and Weaver define attention as "A unified, coordinated muscular set, or attitude, which brings sense organs to bear with maximum effectiveness upon a source of stimulation and thus contributes to alertness and readiness of response."[1] Oliver defines attention as "the process of concentrating the receptive resources of the organism."[2] Many writers use the terms attention and interest together and interchangeably. Whatever we give our attention to must be interesting, and whatever is interesting we will give our attention to. Attention may be defined from two points of view. In the first place, it may be thought of as a bodily *set* or an adjustment of the sensory apparatus, so that we are more keenly sensitive to certain specific stimuli out of the multiplicity of stimuli that impinge upon us. Attention may also be thought of as an increased awareness of certain stimuli, which come into the "focus of consciousness."

In order for us to understand this condition called attention, something must first be known of the span or duration, the selectivity, the kinds, and nature of the stimulus that can create it.

Brembeck and Howell refer to three kinds of attention — involuntary, voluntary and nonvoluntary. In the *involuntary* there are some stimuli to which we must pay attention. They are so strong as to break in on attention already in progress. In the *voluntary*, there are some situations that demand a definite effort to attend. One's own interests may not yet be great enough to remove the effort, so it demands definite voluntary type of attending, and we must force ourselves to attend. In the *nonvoluntary* attention, one's interests are aroused, when stimuli are found to be linked with one's desires, and, consequently, the effort to attend seems to fade away and one attends with pleasure.[3]

William James stated that "what-we-attend-to and what-interests-us are synonymous terms."[4] James Winans agreed that interest and attention are related as cause and effect, and either may be the cause of the other. Winans stated, "It is plain enough that we attend to what interests us; but this restates rather than solves our problem."[5]

William James's theory was that interest grows with knowledge:

> Any object not interesting in itself may become interesting through being associated with an object in which an interest already exists. . . . Associate the new with the old in some natural and telling way, so that the interest, being shed along from point to point, finally suffuses the entire system of objects of thought. . . . The absolutely new is the absolutely uninteresting.[6]

Winans applied James's psychology to public speaking when he stated that interest is strongest in old things or familiar things in new settings, looked at from new angles, given new forms and developed with new facts and ideas, with new light on familiar characters, new explanations of familiar phenomena, or new applications of old truths.[7]

After gaining attention, the next problem is to sustain this initial attention. Psychologists and most of the writers in the field of speech agree that one idea cannot be sustained more than a few seconds. William James wrote:

> There is no such thing as voluntary attention sustained for more than a few seconds at a time. What is called sustained voluntary attention is a repetition of successive efforts which bring the topic back to the mind. . . . No one can possibly attend continuously to an object that does not change. (Quoting Helmholtz) If we wish to keep it upon one and the same object, we must seek constantly to find out something new about the latter, especially if other powerful impressions are attracting us away.[8]

In order to keep a thought alive then, we must keep doing something with it. The span of absolute attention has been found to be only a few seconds. Pillsbury's studies revealed the duration of a single act of attention to be from three to twenty-four seconds, with most acts falling within the five- to eight-second range. Walter Dill Scott years ago observed the brevity of the attention span:

> All of our thinking is done in "spurts," which are uniformly followed by periods of inactivity. We can think of nothing consecutively for any great length of time. What we have called constant or fixed attention is simply spurts of attention, and if we desire to hold it for a longer period of time on an unchangeable object, all we can do is to keep pulling ourselves together repeatedly, and avoid as far as possible all competing thoughts or counter attractions.[9]

He continued with the idea that thoughts that will not develop cannot be attended to for more than a few seconds but thoughts that develop may be attended to for a long period of time, although the attention will not be uniformly strong all the time. In a lecture it is seldom possible that a professor is able to hold the full and undivided attention of the students for more than a few seconds or a very few minutes at best. The hearer's attention is constantly wandering or decreasing in force.

In the business world of the mass media and drama, for example, in the theaters, cinemas and television, the film producers, playwrights, and advertisers have all carefully studied the nature of attention and spent many millions in an effort to capture the attention and interest so that they can manupulate the behavior of their audiences, while many lecturers plod along clumsily, bemoaning the lack of interest in the subject matter they are presenting day after day in a manner that defies or negates all the principles that govern the workings of the human mind!

In order to capture the attention of the students and sustain this initial interest, the professor must, first of all present the subject material in an interesting way until a genuine interest intrinsic to the subject can grow and develop. One of the major theories of interest is Overstreet's principle of "crossing the interest deadline."[10] In all communication there is a certain deadline of interest which must be crossed early by a speaker or writer if the hearers or readers are to remain alert. Successful plays, novels, films, and speeches frequently begin with a situation. We attend to such situations because there usually is movement and activity, or suspense and surprise, etc. Many professors do not begin with their subject material the moment the class bell rings at the beginning of a class period, but rather spend a few moments in well-chosen words to discuss a matter of significant current events or some story of interest, until the students have *settled in* and are *tuning in* to that particular *frequency*. This, if done with care and discretion, can help to bring the listeners over the interest deadline. It is too risky to assume that the students will attend to the professor as the data is gradually and boringly unfolded, eventually revealing that something is being discussed which may be of some concern to them. Overstreet also suggested beginning with an effect needing a cause. Man is a casual-minded creature. When something new enters our range of experience, almost immediately we want to know the cause or causes of such an effect or situation.

REASONS FOR LACK OF INTEREST IN CLASSROOM

There are at least a dozen causes for a lack of interest in many classroom situations. Let us consider a number of these causes briefly.

1. *A dull person teaching the course.* As mentioned in the chapter on personality, one of the reasons for uninteresting, dull teaching is uninteresting, dull teachers, whose living techniques are no

better than their teaching techniques. As Kenneth Eble expressed it plainly in undisguised language, "The boring teacher, the bane of all students is probably fairly bored himself."[11] In almost all students questionnaires in which teaching effectiveness is being evaluated, interest rates high in the list of desired qualifications. Eble enumerated the first three qualities in importance as: (1) The teacher's command of the subject; (2) The teacher's ability to organize, explain, and clarify, and (3) The teacher's ability to arouse and sustain interest.[12]

Brembeck and Howell place the full blame of the lack of attention and interest on the speaker.

> The responsibility of inattentiveness is squarely on the speaker. There is no such thing as an inattentive audience. What the speaker really would have meant was the audience was not attending to him. In such a case, his speech must have been boring, trite, unclear, disorganized, lacking in vital materials, indirect or unanimated. So the audience attended to something else.[13]

It is probably impossible for a student not to pay attention to something. Regardless of what teaching method is used (lecture, discussion, seminar or tutorial), it is the teacher, the living person who determines to the greatest extent as to whether the students will be interested or bored.

2. *Teacher not interested in the subject.* If the teacher is not sure of what he is teaching or is not interested in the subject itself, there will be no particular urgency or enthusiasm to share with the students that which is not felt by the instructor. This attitude will sooner or later be reflected to the students, who are constantly judging their instructors and are very quick to sense this insincerity and lack of interest in the subject matter. Cardinal Newman wrote: "No book can convey the special spirit and delicate peculiarities of its subject with that rapidity and certainty which attend on the sympathy of mind with mind, through the eyes, the look, the accent, and the manner, in casual expressions thrown off at the moment, and the unstudied turns of familiar conversation."[14] The textbook may be dull, but if the instructor is wrapped up in the subject matter his enthusiasm will be contagious.

3. *Teacher not interested in students.* It takes two persons to constitute

a teaching situation and a communicative event. The teacher and the student must give inspiration to each other and receive inspiration from each other. In this teacher-student relationship there must be an exchange of ideas. This emotional situation can exist only when initially the instructor demonstrates genuine interest in the student who then is likely to reciprocate an interest in the instructor as well as the subject being taught. The Purdue Rating Scale, a useful device to assess instructional ability (orginally constructed by Remmers) listed the first two qualities being judged as (1) interest in subject, and (2) sympathetic attitude toward students.

The teacher who has a personal concern for his students duplication and respects them will receive pleasure in watching their progress, and at the same time gain enjoyment from teaching. Having an interest in the subject and in the students constitute the most fundamental assumptions and requirements for good teaching or effective classroom communication. The professor must have initiative and be able to generate curiosity and interest in the subject matter which should be taught creatively.

4. *Teacher not interested in teaching.* Even worse than the teacher not being interested in the subject or the students is the teacher not being interested in teaching. As mentioned in the chapter on personality and dedication, the teacher who is not fully committed to the task of teaching will find very little personal pleasure in the responsibilities of instructing, and, consequently, will exhibit little interest in the classroom. Quintilian asserted that "the orator who wishes to set the people on fire must himself be burning." If this is true of the orator, it is even more important with the teacher who faces the same audience day after day for many weeks.

5. *Teacher using a teaching method for which there is little talent and no training.* This has been dealt with in Chapter 4.

6. *Lecturer reads from a manuscript.* The widely practiced method of delivery of lectures by reading scripts or notes lacks the flexibility of alteration at a moment of inspiration, or when revisions and adaptations become necessary as the result of feedback. The reading of a manuscript can become the greatest single factor in creating a lack of attention and in-

terest. There is absolutely nothing as boring and dull as the poorly written and poorly read manuscript. Even the carefully polished and ordered script can become exceedingly tiresome. Most scripts are written in a formal or bookish, rather than an oral style, and, therefore, lack directness and a sense of communication. It is very difficult to read such a script in a conversational tone. The loss of eye contact constitutes another obvious contributor to a lack of interest and attention in the reading of a manuscript or class notes. Maintaining good eye contact is a most important ingredient in securing and maintaining the attention and interest of the listeners.

Since the attention span is extremely brief, even under the most favorable circumstances, it is apt to fade and become completely nonexistent after as little as two or three minutes of uninteresting reading. The professor who chooses to read lectures to the class risks the loss of the personal touch with the listeners, which is so vital to generating and sustaining attention and interest. The reading of notes or a manuscript can hold the attention and create interest only if written in an oral style, employing descriptive imagery and picturesque figures of speech, and when read by a person with either native ability or training in the art of oral interpretation.

7. *The instructor does not properly motivate the students.* This will be fully discussed in a later chapter.

8. *No definite purpose or organization.* In the last chapter this matter of lack of purpose and organization was elaborated upon, and it is obvious that if the professor rambles on, there is no real sense or meaning to what is being said. Unless the students can follow the ideas, without exerting an undue amount of energy in *voluntary* attention, their interest will readily shift to some other stimuli.

9. *The teacher does not put forth a conscious attempt to hold the attention of students.* Since communication is impossible without attention, and since the attention span toward any given stimulus is relatively brief, effective teaching depends upon the skillful use of every technique and rhetorical device that will compel legitimately the attention of every member of the class. Some of the *factors of attention* that will aid the teacher in maintaining interest follow.

FACTORS OF ATTENTION

Alan Monroe listed nine qualities of subject matter that usually capture the spontaneous attention of the listeners: (1) activity or movement, (2) reality, (3) proximity, (4) familiarity, (5) novelty, (6) suspense, (7) conflict, (8) humor, and (9) the vital. There is an overlapping in these and often several are combined in an effort to hold the attention of the listeners.[15]

Activity and Movement

In order to create interest and sustain attention there must be activity and movement, variety and change, or else there may be stagnation and dullness. We have often heard it said that variety is the spice of life. How can this factor of attention be brought into the college and university classroom? There are a number of ways in which the professor can utilize movement. During the presentation of a lecture there should be progression of thoughts and ideas in the unfolding of a well-ordered sequence. It should move along from one point to the next in logical fashion with proper transitions between each major idea. McLeish tells of students who were "caught up" with lectures of distinguished teachers. They were "involved and participated in a measure in the thought-processes of the lecturer. Students experienced, if only at second-hand, the excitement of discovery. For a short time at any rate, it was as though they were in the front-line of intellectual advance, at the very frontiers of knowledge."[16]

Another way to bring variety into the class period is to vary the auditory by asking questions, introducing brief duscussions or dialogue. The auditory should be supplemented with the visual. Explain and illustrate or even demonstrate a difficult point by the use of visual aids. The following types of visual aids are available to the instructor: the actual object, working model, pictures of the objects, graphs, charts, the blackboard (to draw or illustrate or duplicate an outline), overhead projector or slides, and movie films.

A few guiding principles for the use of visual aids are the following:

1. Make certain the visual aid is large enough for everyone to see.

2. Place the visual aid in the best position so that each student can see it.
3. Keep the visual aid out of sight until ready to use.
4. Remove the visual aid as soon as finished using it.
5. Don't speak to the visual aid.
6. Practice the lecture with the use of the visual aid.
7. Keep talking to the class while displaying the visual aid.
8. When using the blackboard, do not turn your back completely to the class, and do not stand in front of the blackboard material.

Another aspect of variety and change relates to the voice as will be discussed in a later chapter. Sameness in rate, pitch, volume, and quality results in monotony, which breeds dullness, whereas vocal variety in these areas stimulates interest and arouses attention. The teacher can also utilize movement and activity through gestures. One must, however, avoid the sameness in this activity by varying the types of gestures used. Gestures help to communicate ideas, and for this reason alone they would create interest, but, furthermore, since gestures involve motion of the hands, arms and shoulders they-necessitate a change in position, and this activity in itself invokes attention. Gestures and bodily movements should, of course, always be meaningful and not employed merely for the purpose of gaining attention.

Reality

A good way to lose the interest of the listener is to speak in abstract terms and vague generalizations. How often do we hear advertisers say, "Experts across the country agree. . . ." Who are these *experts*? Where do they live and practice? Do they actually all agree on all points? Individual cases are more real then general classifications. Descriptions must be specific and vivid in order to hold attention. Begin with the concrete and specific examples before going on to the abstract and general.

Proximity

In general, people are interested in that which is close in time and space. A horrible act of genocide in twelfth century China is of comparatively little interest, but the accident that took the life of one child a day before in the local village becomes vastly more significant. This principle of nearness or *proximity* can create at least temporary interest when a reference is made to an individual in the class, but this singling out of a person or persons within the group can be overdone. Making the subject matter of the course relevant to the life and present situations in which the students themselves are involved constitutes another way of employing the factor of attention, referred to as proximity.

Familiarity

We feel more comfortable with things that are familiar to us, and we are quite reticent about accepting ideas and plans that are new and different. Relating new or unfamiliar material to what is already known and understood is one of the best methods of instruction. Henderson commented on this well-known maxim or teaching principle of proceeding from the known to the unknown, as well as working from simple concepts to more complex ones:

> We learn by building on old material. The effective lecturer, therefore, presents his new ideas strictly in relation to the group's previous knowledge. Students must be prepared for their new learning to link each new lesson with its predecessor in some way. The process of associating ideas and enlarging meaning takes place at all stages in learning. Guard against the sudden introduction of new concepts and unfamiliar words into a lecture. . . . Expressed in terms of a maxim, this means you must root all new teaching, in familiar related material.
>
>   . . . proceed from uncomplicated and first-known ideas to the more complex thought-systems derived from them. . . . By using simplified examples, you enhance the interest of students ensuring better learning from the outset.[17]

It is most difficult, if not almost impossible, to keep one's attention focused upon an idea or concept that is entirely new and completely unfamiliar. On the other hand, a person soon loses interest and becomes bored by the repetition of that which is old and familiar.

Novelty

Novelty is another factor of attention which can become a potent force in arousing attention when the old ideas and factual materials are presented in different (as well as interesting) ways. It must, however, not be presented in an entirely new and different way so that it becomes largely unfamiliar. There should be a balance between the familiar and the novel.

Suspense

Another technique that will help ward off the monster of dullness is suspense. This factor of attention could be employed at the beginning of the class period by the use of a rhetorical question or series of questions to which the answers can be explicitly given or strongly implied later in the lecture. Suspense cannot be maintained unduly long before it is resolved, otherwise the listeners will finally give up and lose interest. The resolving of the suspense must also be commensurate to the degree and duration of the suspense, or else the hearers will feel cheated for having been suspended in midair for relatively little real reward for all of their tension and anticipation.

Humor

It is seldom justifiable for a teacher to take up considerable time during class to tell humorous anecdotes for the sole purpose of evoking laughter. When people laugh it indicates that they are enjoying themselves, and people will pay attention to that which they enjoy. There is nothing like an occasional funny story or joke to capture the attention of the students in the class, especially if the material being presented is somewhat abstract or difficult to comprehend. Humor provides relaxation. Humor in the classroom, however, serves the purpose of teaching best when it is relevant to the thoughts which the instructor is endeavoring to develop, if it is in good taste and inoffensive, and if it is not at someone else's expense.

Conflict

A clash of opinions always arrests attention and instantly creates interest, especially concerning issues in which the students can agree with one of the contending sides. I have often resorted to assigning students to prepare speeches on the opposite sides of a controversial topic, or present conflicting views in a discussion or even a debate. When a student presents one viewpoint, many of the fellow class members can hardly wait until they are given a chance for a rebuttal, and this usually ends up in a lively discussion.

Another effective way of utilizing conflict as an element of interest and attention is for the professor to set up an argument during the first part of the lecture and then knock it down further along in the lecture period. Conflict, like suspense, must be satisfactorily resolved in due course.

The Vital

People will pay attention to those things which directly and immediately affect their lives and their security. If the instructor can convince the students that the subject matter of the course concerns them personally, and if the course can be related to their interests and needs they will consider it of vital importance and listen more intently.

To sum up the matter of a conscious attempt of the speaker to continually attract the attention of the listeners, Monroe wrote the following:

> Attention, as we have emphasized, is *unstable* and *impermanent*. Focus tends to come and to go, and your listeners' internal and external perceptual fields are under a steady bombardment from a variety of stimuli. When preparing and presenting a speech, therefore, do not assume that all you need to do is catch the attention of your listeners in the first moments of your discourse. As your message proceeds, your audience's attention will ebb and flow, peak and lag. Consequently, you must be concerned throughout your speech — in the opening, closing, and at all points in between — with recapturing your listeners' attention and bringing it back again and again to the ideas you wish to communicate.[18]

PATTERNS OF STUDENT CLASSROOM ATTENTION

D.H. Lloyd of the University of Reading, Berkshire, England, conducted an experiment on effective communication during periods of student attention. He reasoned that the amount of knowledge assimilated by a student in a lecture depended largely upon two factors: the lecturer's transmittal performance or the capacity of a lecturer to present information in assimilable form, and the students' receptivity or the normal capacity of a student at a specific time to receive and comprehend information. Assimilation is the direct function of the knowledge derived by the student resulting from transmittal performance and receptivity. During this experiment two lectures were given in which the teaching notes were kept as constant as possible in pace, stimulus, intellectual difficulty and manner of presentation. Lloyd formulated a graph or contour which illustrates his findings. These findings indicated that there is a sudden rise in attention after the initial *settling in* period, after which there is a constant decline of attention and assimilation until just before the end of the lecture at which time attention picks up again suddenly and then diminshes sharply at the very end of the class period. He divided the fifty-minute class period into the following six sections describing the attention during each period.

0- 5 min. A period of mutual adjustment and mutual stimulation between lecturer and class. The class is at its physical and mental receptive peak. The lecturer is at his transmission peak. Full communication is not initially established and hence assimilation is sub-optimal but improves rapidly.

5-10 min. Adjustment achieved and communication at maximum. Sustained peak performance by lecturer and class. Assimilation at its highest.

10-20 min. A period of progressive tiring of the lecturer and class accompanied by mental confusion and boredom amongst students. Receptivity of the class falls rapidly. Transmittal power of lecturer also falls but less severely. Assimilation falls rapidly.

20-40 min. A period of low activity caused by partial exhaustion of lecturer and class boredom of students. Transmittal power usually well above receptivity, probably because of the stimulus to continued effort received by the lecturer, due to his active personal participation. Assimilation weak.

40-45 min. Revived activity amongst the class due to stimulus of approaching relief in terms of closure of lecture — receptivity rises sharply. Lecturer's transmittal power continues to fall due to increasing tiredness and infection by the class's prior insensitivity. Assimilation improves but remains low.

45-50 min. Revived activity and increased transmittal power from the

lecturer, who is now stimulated by the approach of the end
of his activity and also infected by the recent increased sensitivity of the students.

A rapid fall occurs in the class's receptivity due to impa-
tience for the closure of the lecture and anticipation of, and
thought transference to, impending activities. Assimilation
by the class at its lowest level.[19]

Lloyd allowed for some variations and modifications in the basic
contour of the above attention pattern, as a result of such factors as
interest, content of the subject, mood or personality of the lecturer,
mood of the students, as well as such factors as room comfort, time
of the day, week or term (i.e. just before exams).

A later experiment conducted by Dr. A.H. Johnstone and F. Percival added to the information already provided by Lloyd, McLeish,
and others. The experiment involved twelve lecturers in ninety lectures, mostly first-year courses in chemistry, and was carried out
with the aim of finding some evidence for the existence and frequency of periods of nonattention. The observers at these lectures
noted signs of nonattention, not so much in a smooth curve, but that
there were general attention breaks or *microsleeps*, as Bligh labeled
them, when the mind "wanders or is stimulated to explore some relevant issue."[20] It was also noted that these attention breaks increased
with time during a lecture. The first period of nonattention generally came ten to eighteen minutes later, and as the lecture continued
the attention span grew shorter until towards the end of the lecture
period the attention span was decreased to three or four minutes.

Some of the lecturers in the experiment broke up the class sessions with short films, brief discussions etc., and the students were
allowed to relax mentally during these variations. The assumption
was that "learning time lost in providing variation in a lecture was
more than recouped in terms of student learning."[21]

In McLeish's studies, as mentioned in an earlier chapter, the
Trenaman and Norwich experiments concerning the ability to concentrate throughout a fifty-minute period revealed that students
were able to copy down in their notes and take away in their minds
41 percent of a fifteen minute talk, 25 percent of a thirty-minute portion of a lecture, and only 20 percent of what was said during forty-
five minutes, which indicates that the attention levels decline during

a lecture "as it is commonly delivered."[22]

Coats and Smidchens of the School of Education at the University of Michigan conducted an experiment a number of years ago, which inferred that a dynamic lecture delivery is more successful than a static one in eliciting and maintaining the attention of a class. The hypothesis for their study was that "students will remember more from a given lecture when the delivery is dynamic than when it is static."[23] The study involved 184 students in eight fundamental speech classes. The lectures were expository in nature and of identical content. Four speeches were given by each of the two speakers. Two were delivered with a dynamic presentation — with vocal variety, animation and enthusiasm, etc., and the other lectures were read from a manuscript. The *static* speaker used no gestures or direct eye contact and had very little vocal inflection. The *dynamic* speeches were delivered from memory and the speaker used much vocal inflection, gestures, eye contact and animation. Immediately following each lecture the dynamism scale was used to measure audience perception of the speaker's dynamism. The data that emerged from this study "very convincingly supported the major hypothesis that students remember much more from the dynamic lecture than from the static one." Coats and Smidchens further concluded:

> Such a finding has strong implications for both practice and future research. The work and planning, which are requisite to effective dynamic speaking, are evidently rewarded with a high degree of audience attention. The relation which was demonstrated to exist between speaker dynamism and audience attention might be considered by teachers.[24]

The overall conclusion of the "Dr. Fox" experiment seemed to connote that the lecturer to a great extent is responsible for the interest or lack of it in the classroom. As mentioned earlier, Michael Fox, a Hollywood actor was hired to produce six videotaped lectures. Three lectures, differing only in content density (high, medium, and low), were delivered in both high and low-expressive manners. To achieve this "high expressive" manner, "Dr. Fox" employed many of the factors of attention — humor, movement, enthusiasm, friendliness, charisma, and personality, as well as voice modulation to embellish these lectures. "Student ratings of lectures high in expressiveness exceeded ratings of low-expressive lectures and in that respect corresponded with achievement results."[25]

There are those who have used "Dr. Fox" and his experiments as proof of the hypnotic influence in manipulating the behavior of others through the oratory and the dramatic arts. Like every other legitimate art that is employed to enrich our lives and culture in general, they can be misused for unethical ends, and this is what we see in the *Dr. Fox Effect* as it is referred to, in which case the *form* is so attractive that the listener is charmed into believing the *content*. In the book, *Lecturecraft*, Cockburn and Ross described another experiment involving the actor Michael Fox.

> Dr. Fox was an actor who rehearsed and delivered a lecture to audiences of experienced educators on a manufactured topic by no means beyond the reach of the professional judgment. Their lecture deliberately contained an excessive amount of double talk, neologisms, non-sequiturs and contradictory statements, but it was delivered with warmth, panache, enthusiasm, humor and meaningless references to unrelated topics. It went down well and over half were seduced. "Dr. Fox" was congratulated; one member of an audience even recalled "Dr. Fox's " non-existent publication.[26]

Cockburn and Ross left this warning to any professor who might be trained or talented in communicative skills. "Histrionic skill can be counterproductive. The gifted should rein themselves in and beware of careening after Foxes!" Their final conclusion was that "performance may be a crutch to the idle and a disguise for an inadequate lecture."[27]

As stated earlier, we are not dealing with an either-or situation, as though we had only two alternatives to choose from or to imitate: that of an actor comedian (or clown) or extrovert glib performer, as opposed to a disseminator or dispenser of knowledge with a take-it-or-leave-it attitude. The main concern of the professor should be neither with expounding nor with entertaining.

Max Marshall felt that often professors are too concerned with trying to present the subject matter in an interesting manner, and in doing so they may actually be diverting interest from the subject itself. He placed the matter of interest as a responsibility of the individual student. In an article entitled "Is It Interesting?" Marshall asked the question, "Are teachers actors or explicators?" to which he added, "That question can arouse many frenzied answers."[28] He is not necessarily referring to actors like Michael, but the ordinary professor who is putting forth an effort to arrest the attention of the students and create an interest in the subject material and the class in general. Marshall caricatures these *actors* in the following graphic description. "Because of their enthusiasm and empathy with students, starry-eyed teachers themselves seek to assume the responsibility for interesting students."[29] This enthusiasm and empathy or "bubbling personality" is here condemned, because it not only blocks interest in the subject matter but allegedly becomes a detriment to learning. "But teachers who, with bubbling personalities or excessive effort, divert attention from the learning process may have even a reverse effect on the interest of students, at least in the subject."[30]

In an effort to place the teacher somewhere between the two extremes of explicator or actor, Marshall places more responsibility upon the student in the matter of generating interest in the subject material. "Actors who divert, mistaking entertainment for interest, and the full-fledged explicator, do the thinking for students, one by diversion, the other by drowing interest. . . . A qualified teacher uses the subject itself as bait to fish for interest, not dramatic entertainment. The fish in the pond may be hungry, or they may be fearful and reluctant to take the bait, the subject, but the student and the subject have to come together."[31]

I would go one step further and state that in this analogy one would have to admit that the wise fisherman will bait his hook only with that which is considered by the fish as tasty and palatable in order to attract the attention of the fish and to get the fish in contact with the bait.

Without interest there is no attention, and without attention there can be no learning. Lack of attention and interest result in a partial or complete breakdown in classroom communication.

NOTES

1. O'Neill, James Milton, and Weaver, Andrew Thomas: *Elements of Speech.* (rev. ed.) New York, Longmans, 1933, p. 249.
2. Oliver, Robert T.: *The Psychology of Persuasive Speech,* 2nd ed. New York, Longmans, Green and Co., 1957, p. 118.
3. Brembeck, Winston L., and Howell, William S.: *Persuasion — A Means of Social Control.* New York, Prentice-Hall, 1952, p. 276. (*see* Chapter 10).

4. Winans, James Albert: Public Speaking, P. 53. Quoting William James, *Psychology: Briefer Course*, p. 448.
5. Winans, James Albert: *Public Speaking*. New York, The Century Co., 1917, pp. 53, 54.
6. James, William: *Talks to Teachers*. New York, Henry Holt and Co., 1912, p. 94.
7. Winans, James Albert: *Public Speaking*. pp. 57-59.
8. James, William,: *Psychology*. New York, H. Holt and Co., 1904, p. 224.
9. Scott, Walter Dill: *Psychology of Public Speaking*. New York, Noble and Nobel Publishers, 1926, pp. 112, 113.
10. Overstreet, Henry Allen: *Influencing Human Behavior, W. W. Norton & Co., Inc., 1925, pp. 110-124.*
11. *Eble, Kenneth E.: Professors as Teachers.* San Francisco, Jossey-Bass Inc., 1972, p. 48.
12. Eble, Kenneth E.: *Professors as Teachers*. p. 66.
13. Brembeck and Howell: *Persuasion — A Means of Social Control*. p. 276. Also Monroe, Alan H., and Ehninger, Douglas: *Principles and Types of Speech*, 6th ed. Glenview, Scott, Foresman, 1967, p. 209.
14. Barzun, Jacques: *We Who Teach*. London, Victor Gollancz, Ltd., 1946, p. 37, quoting Cardinal Newman.
15. Monroe, Alan H. and Ehninger, Douglas: *Principles and Types of Speech*, 6th ed. Glenview, Scott, Foresman, 1967, p. 210.
16. McLeish, John: *The Lecture Method*. Cambridge, Cambridge Institute of Education, 1968, Heffers of Cambridge, Printers, p. 42.
17. Henderson, Norman K.: *University Teaching*. Hong Kong, Hong Kong University Press, 1969 (through Oxford University Press), p. 16.
18. Ehninger, Douglas, Monroe, Alan H., and Gronbeck, Bruce E.: *Principles and Types of Speech Communication*, 8th ed. Glenview, Scott, Foresman and Co., 1978, pp. 135, 136.
19. Lloyd, D.H.: Communication in the university lecture. *University of Reading Staff Journal, No. 1*:20, February, 1967. Reading, England, University of Reading Pub.
20. Bligh, Donald A.: *What's the Use of Lectures?* Exeter, D.A. and B. Bligh Pub., University Teaching Methods Unit, 1971, p. 66.
21. Johnstone, A.H., and Percival, F.: Attention breaks in lectures, *Education in Chemistry, 13, No. 2*:49, 50, March, 1976.
22. McLeish, John: *The Lecture Method*. p. 6ff.
23. Coats, William D., and Smidchens, Uldis: Audience recall as a function of speaker dynamism. *Journal of Educational Psychology, 57, No. 4*:191, 1966.
24. Coats, William D., and Smidchens, Uldis: Audience recall as a function of speaker dynamism. p. 191.
25. Williams, Reed G., and Ware, John E. Jr.: Validity of student ratings of instruction under different incentive conditions: a further study of the Dr. Fox effect. *Journal of Educational Psychology, 68, No. 1*:48, 50, 1976.
26. Cockburn, Barbara, and Ross, Alec: *Lecturecraft*. Lancaster, University of Lancaster, 1977, p. 56.

27. Cockburn, Barbara, and Ross, Alec: *Lecturecraft.* p. 56.
28. Marshall, Max S.: Is it interesting? *Improving College and University Teaching, Vol. 21*:17, 1973.
29. Marshall, Max S.: Is it interesting? p. 17.
30. Marshall, Max S.: Is it interesting? p. 17.
31. Marshall, Max S.: Is it interesting? p. 18.

CHAPTER 7

DELIVERING THE LECTURE

Speech is a basic tool, the chief means by which teachers attempt to reach students, and command of voice is as serviceable a part of professional competence as command of subject matter.
Kenneth Eble

A mediocre speech supported by all the power of delivery will be more impressive than the best speech unaccompanied by such power.
Quintilian

AS stated in the last chapter, one of the greatest barriers to classroom communication is the lack of interest and attention. Without attention there can be no interest; subsequently, very little, if any, real learning can take place. Attracting attention and sustaining interest depend upon competence in other areas of the communicative process, and as noted earlier, these are intricately linked with every other aspect of communication. Poor delivery constitutes one of the greatest causes for a lack of attention and interest, and, consequently, it undoubtedly is directly responsible for creating another major breakdown in classroom communication.

The matter of delivery raises the age-old question that has come down to us from the days of the classical rhetoricians of Greece and

Rome — which is more important, content or form? It should never have been an either-or situation and a question of matter versus manner, or whether *what* is said is more important than *how* it is said. These two aspects are related, and each is important; there is no good reason why they cannot be found in the same presentation. They do not constitute a mutually exclusive dichotomy: it is not that one finds either flowery speech or oratory lacking in content; or significant content material unadulterated with any frills and embellishment.

Eble considered good delivery to be as important as the teacher's knowledge of subject material.

> Speech is a basic tool, the chief means by which teachers attempt to reach students, and command of voice is as serviceable a part of professional competence as command of subject matter. If an effective manner of speaking must be worked at, so must any other aspect of professional competence, and the work necessary to bringing voice qualities to acceptable levels requires but a fraction of the time customarily given to gaining mastery of a discipline. Teachers should obviously have voice qualities and direction that are reasonably effective — even pleasing — to others. Persons proposing to earn a living by using their voices have obligations to develop force and control and to overcome stridencies, nasalities, and the like.[1]

During the past four or five decades, many articles have been written listing and enumerating the individual qualities or set of standards composing criteria for effective teaching in higher education. It is assumed that any single, or combination of all of these characteristics and prerequisites for effective teaching, have a direct connection to the aims and objectives of teaching, namely, the student's ability to understand course material, and learn to think for himself and apply learning to actual life situations. Attempts have been made to determine which is the most significant of these qualities. Lita Schwartz, consultant editor of *Improving College and University Teaching* voiced her opinion (and, undoubtedly, that of many other educators) as to what ability or trait in the teacher constitutes the prime significant factor for effective teaching. "Effective teaching presumably results in effective learning . . . there have been numerous attempts to analyze 'effective teaching' so that it can be handled objectively. Of all the factors listed in attempts at quantitative analysis, the outstanding one is the ability to communicate effectively."[2]

By "ability to communicate" she meant clarity of speech, but she also included organization of the material and style of presentation in an effort to stimulate thinking. Lita Schwartz then concluded that this ability is essential in any teaching method, but particularly so in the lecture-discussion method. In the following statement she pointed out this obvious relationship: "Since the dominant teaching technique in higher education today continues to be the lecture-discussion method, especially in lower-division courses, the importance of communication is self-evident."[3]

This high regard for the teacher's ability to communicate effectively is not, however, shared by all educators. Instead of taking the positive position expressed years ago by T.H. Pear ("The technique of imparting knowledge in the special way called lecturing can be learned and improved upon,"), and believing that one way in which it obviously could be improved is through the mastery of oral communication, some have followed a false line of argument. This chain of "reasoning" is (a) Lectures "as they are commonly delivered" are less effective than other methods for most objectives, (b) Public speaking and communication skills are largely the concerns of the lecture method, (c) Therefore, the time and effort needed to develop communication skills are not worthwhile and this time and effort can be more profitably spent on other teaching methods.

In an article entitled "An Assessment of the Lecture," the authors came to just such a conclusion: the well-prepared lecture is not worth the effort that the lecturer has to put into it. "It seemed that the benefit of a well-prepared and delivered lecture (assuming that this were done) might not be worth the time and effort that went with it, and that the student might learn and retain more information from teaching methods such as seminars, laboratories, or on his own. As a teaching tool unto itself, its value relative to expenditure of time and effort is still in question."[4]

Those who express their attitudes about speech in similar opinions are guilty of making the following two erroneous assumptions: (1) public speaking is an end in itself; and (2) although speech is of primary importance in lecturing, it is of comparatively little significance in the use of other teaching methods.

The ability to communicate orally is not an end in itself. It is the vehicle in the interchange of thoughts and ideas in the learning process and intellectual development of the student. Good communication is an indication of good thinking. The emphasis in the chapter and, indeed, throughout the entire book is on the lecture method or combination of the lecture and discussion technique. The rhetorical principles discussed here apply mainly to the most widely used teaching method, which is the only feasible method in many colleges and universities where economy and other factors dictate that teachers lecture. Some modifications must, of necessity, be made in other teaching methods, as Arthur Wise pointed out:

> In considering speech as communication, we must remind ourselves that such speech takes place in a particular situation. That situation qualifies that speech. Speech which is successful in one situation can be useless in another. The speech of the lecture theatre is totally inappropriate to the tutorial situation. To be successful, speech behavior must be adjusted to the terms of reference of the situation in which it is being used.[5]

Regardless of what teaching method is used, the teacher talks during a considerable portion of the time in any type of classroom teaching, and it is, therefore, important for the instructor to know how to use voice, diction and the body correctly in verbal and non-verbal communication.

It may not be necessary for a teacher to have the resonance and force of an orator, or the impeccable enunciation and correct pronunciation of a television announcer, or the quick wit of a popular master of ceremony, but this does not give license to be as boring and dry as the proverbial hills of Gilboa, or to speak indistinctly and inaudibly, using distracting mannerisms and annoying pet expressions, punctuated with frequent pauses and space fillers as *er, ahs,* or *you know*. In shunning artificiality and display, the teacher need not freeze in emotive expressions or convey an attitude of apathy or downright disinterest, lacking in eye contact, vocal flexibility and bodily activity, and maintaining a static cold reserve or psychological distance. There is no reason why students should have to strain to hear the professor, nor should they be unsure of what they manage to hear. Students should not become weary in a frustrating attempt to stay awake or become exhausted in their efforts to follow closely a lecture or discussion-lecture in which no points stand out in importance because of a lack of bodily and vocal emphasis.

Every teacher, regardless of the particular teaching situation should be aware of, and be able to put into practice effectively, the rhetorical principles of delivery. Delivery consists of the verbal and nonverbal messages employed to convey words and meaning by the speaker to the listeners. While the professor is teaching he is actually sending out three messages simultaneously. Two of these stimuli are produced by the voice, and one is transmitted by movements of the body. First of all, the listener hears the actual word symbols as they are vocalized, and instantly must not only hear, but must understand and interpret each word or group of words. The second set of stimuli relate to the way in which those words are spoken. The four aspects of vocal expression are rate, inflection, volume, and quality. The listener must hear these changes and be sensitive to the various shades of meaning they are intended to transmit. The third set of stimuli, making up the total message, involves the bodily movements and gestures. The listener must see and observe these stimuli while he is hearing and interpreting the words and vocal changes. According to medical science, there are specialized areas in the cerebral cortex and cerebellum which not only direct the production of articulate speech, but which perceive and interpret auditory speech sounds and (in separate lobes) process visual symbols. The entire communication process from the speaker to the listener and feedback to the speaker is most complex.

Quintilian stated that "all delivery is concerned with two different things, namely voice and gesture, of which one appeals to the eye and the other to the ear, the two senses by which all emotion reaches the soul. But the voice has the first claim on our attention, since even our gesture is adapted to suit it."[6]

Classroom communication consists of three elements: the *verbal* — the word symbols that are spoken which represent the thoughts and ideas; *vocal* — the sound qualities of the voice, conveying meaning and connotations; and the *visible* — the reinforcement of the meaning of the words, conveyed to the listener by seeing the movements and gestures of the teacher. While the teacher is talking, delivery becomes an act of producing audible, visible, and verbal symbols all at the same moment. Classroom communication is an activity that involves the body, or the *physiological* element; a variety of the sounds or noises interspersed with pauses, or the *acoustical* element; and the seeing and interpreting of movements, or the *ocular* element. There is actually a fourth element in delivering a lecture or partaking in a discussion, which may in fact be the result of combining all three of the other elements — the emotional or *psychological* element, because the entire personality of the teacher enters into the act of teaching.

Teaching, which is lacking in any one of these elements of delivery, reduces the effectiveness of communicating, and, therefore, communication breakdown can be due to a lack or improper use of any one or the combination of all of these elements. This chapter deals primarily with the verbal and nonverbal aspects of communication.

THE TEACHER'S VOICE

Let us first consider the teacher's voice. As mentioned earlier, as a professional person whose main function depends upon the voice, it is assumed that one of the obvious qualifications of a teacher is the possession of a pleasing resonant voice.

Most of us are seldom conscious of how we sound to others. We take our speech for granted just as we do our manner of walking. It has become a definite and inseparable part of our personality. Do you remember hearing your voice for the first time, as it was played back on a tape recorder or disc? Can you recall your initial impression and your surprise (or shock!)? Probably your first reaction was, "Do I really sound like that!" Yes, that is the way you sound day after day, year after year to those around you. We cannot receive and interpret the physical properties of our own voice as well as our auditors, because we are accustomed to hearing the sounds of our own voice through bone conduction, instead of air conduction.

Communication in the classroom will definitely be impaired if the tone of our voice indicates attitudes of timidity as in a weak and thin voice; aggressiveness or even hatred, as in a harsh, rough voice; effeminateness and lack of confidence (or authority) in a high-pitched tone; dullness in a monotonous voice lacking variety; sophistication, insincerity and aloofness or ostentation, characterized by affected tones and artificial overresonance. Any of these faults plus many others, such as a nasal twang or other unpleasant voice qualities (or lack of quality) can *turn off* the listeners.

The mass media of communication (radio and television) have made people very voice conscious. Many children and adults listen to radio and hear and watch television for as long as five to seven hours or longer every day. It is estimated that at least 50 percent of all radio and television programs consist of the spoken word, much of which is produced by professional speakers (although much of it is a reflection and imitation of *street talk* as in dramatized shows). Nevertheless, even the uneducated and untrained recognize the models of good speech and are inclined to classify people in the social and intellectual scale by the quality of the voice and manner of speaking.

Anything about the presentation of the subject matter that distracts from the content and meaning of that message and calls attention to itself should be avoided. Certainly this is true of the teacher's voice. If the students are attracted to the voice of the instructor and say, "What a beautiful voice the professor has," the teacher has distracted the listener's attention from the most vital part of communication — the transmission of thought. When the teacher becomes more concerned with *how* he speaks than with the message of the words and meaning he is trying to communicate, the voice, instead of being a tool *of* communication becomes a barrier *to* communication. The best speaking voice should neither irritate and annoy the listener, nor exaggerate the good vocal qualities to the point of conspicuousness.

What Thonssen and Baird wrote about the public speaking situation applies also to the classroom speaking:

> An important public speech is not a satisfactory laboratory for testing a speaker's orotund qualities and pleasing cadences. Once the speaker takes the floor to develop an idea, we have a right to expect a lively enforcement of his thoughts. He is there to communicate something worth passing on. Delivery serves as a tool by which to enhance the impressiveness of the communication; it is not the focus of attention.[7]

MECHANICS OF VOICE PRODUCTION

There are four phases necessary in the production of speech —

respiration, vibration, resonation, and articulation. It takes air to produce speech, but many teachers have developed wrong habits of breathing. Diaphragmatic action is required for proper speaking and projection. This action is referred to as a *human air pump*, which works in the following ways:

> Certain muscles draw the ribs down and in when you exhale, so as to squeeze the lungs like the motion of a bellows, while others — the strong abdominal muscles — squeeze in below to exert pressure up against the bottom of the lungs like the motion of a piston. This double action is also exerted when you inhale: One set of muscles pulls the ribs up and out to expand the horizontal space, while the diagraphm — a layer of muscles and flat tendon tissue — expands the vertical space by lowering the floor of the chest cavity. This two-way expansion creates a suction, so that air rushes into the lungs.[8]

Within the larynx, stretched between the cartilages, are the vocal folds. The compressed air from the lungs presses against the vocal folds, causing a vibration that produces sound. This sound is further resonated in the air chambers in the throat, mouth, and sinuses in the cheek bones, forehead, and nasal cavities. Finally, the sounds that have been produced and amplified are broken up by the articulators — the tongue, lips, teeth, jaw, hard and soft palates — into plosive, fricative (hissing), or nasal sounds of the consonants, interspersed by the relatively free flow of air in the production of the vowel sounds. A good speaking voice is characterized by the proper usage of these four areas, resulting in diaphragmatic breathing, relaxed throat, ample amount of resonation and flexible articulators.

Any inadequacies in one or more of these four phases of correct voice production creates a sufficient cause for a communicative barrier. Shallow breathing results in insufficient volume and breathiness or frequent and unnecessary pauses in speaking. Tense vocal chords produce a high-pitched and thin-sounding voice. Clogged resonating chambers or the nonuse of these head cavities produces denasality, or the overuse of these results in nasality. If the articulators are not flexible, the consequences will be displayed in carelessness and sloppy articulation or in lack of clarity of speech sounds.

VOCAL VARIETY

Even though all four of the phases in the mechanics of voice production are correctly executed, it is still possible to have voice barriers to communication. The sounds of the voice may be dull and monotonous. There must be variety in the voice for the following three reasons: (1) to hold the attention of the listeners, (2) to transmit all of the shades of meaning intended, and (3) for emphasis — to make certain words and ideas stand out. All of these purposes may be accomplished by varying the rate, pitch, volume, and quality.

Rate of Speaking

The rate of speaking contributes to the meaning that is being transmitted. Rate can be varied by the change of the overall speed that is appropriate to the content of the thoughts and ideas being expressed. For example, excitement or enthusiasm can be portrayed by a more rapid rate of utterance. The rate of speaking can also be varied by meaningful pauses and by stretching out certain words (or by slowing down) to make these words stand out. The voice that does not vary is a voice that does not communicate or sustain interest.

The rate of speaking is important not only in relation to attention and interest but also in the matter of comprehension. If the rate of speaking is too slow, the students will lose interest in what is being said, but on the other hand, if it is too rapid, they will not be able to follow and comprehend the thoughts being expressed, or take proper notes on what is being said. In either case, communication is hampered, if not altogether halted. The speed in which a lecturer speaks should be determined by the nature and difficulty of the subject material in relation to the student's ability. Ruth Beard and Donald suggested that the speed should vary inversely with the difficulty of material. This principle is consistent with common sense and also consistent with an experiment by Bligh (1974) in which he gave identical lectures to three groups at different speeds.

> Results of multiple choice tests at eight cognitive levels showed significant interaction between speed and subject matter on questions requiring more thought, but differences at lower cognitive levels and for speed alone were not significant. There was a critical speed and level of . . . difficulty at which increases in speed made a crucial difference.[9]

For most individuals the average rate of speaking is 140 to 160 words per minute, but the teacher must gauge the rate in accordance with the complexity of the subject and the ability of the students to comprehend, but a specified rate of speech should not be maintained for any great length of time, lest a monotone pattern develops.

Change of Inflection

A change in pitch or inflection reflects various attitudes and moods; consequently, it is very important to communicating meaning. A voice that does not have adequate inflection is a voice that is dull, uninteresting, and colorless, and one that is very restricted in conveying intended meanings. This lack of proper pitch or inflection becomes another, in the long list of barriers to communication in the classroom. For many teachers this seems to be one of the most difficult of all of the aspects of vocal variety to develop effectively. The natural pitch level of each individual is determined by the length of the vocal chords and other physiological construction, and there is not much that can be done to alter the general pitch. One should not acquire an artificial inflection. A tense, nervous person can strain the voice unless the larynx and throat muscles are relaxed. Most individuals, however, do not utilize their full natural or optimum pitch, and it is within this full range of "notes" that all the various attudes and meanings can be portrayed. Inflection can be upward or downward. In asking a question the voice usually glides upward, and the downward glide often designates positiveness. Upward inflection often indicates indecision and indefiniteness, whereas downward inflections imply decisiveness and definiteness. Concerning the effect of inflection in the classroom, Fessenden et al. wrote:

> Persons who speak with a general pattern of upward inflection are generally thought of as being less dominant than those whose speech is of a general downward inflectional pattern. Constant upward inflections create nervousness and excitement, whereas downward inflections create determination and quietness. Good speech requires a variation in inflectional patterns. The inferior speaker usually has much narrower [sic] range of inflection in his voice than does the superior speaker. Classroom discipline has, on occasions, been related to the teacher's inflectional pattern.[10]

Proper Volume

If the teacher speaks with too much volume, it will annoy the students whose attention will be drawn to the force of the voice, rather than the meaning of the thoughts being expressed. If the volume, however, is too soft, the students will have to strain to hear, and even then not all of the words necessary to understand the complete ideas may be heard, thus causing a partial or complete breakdown in communication. Not only should the volume be adequately loud enough to be heard and understood, but the teacher must gauge the loudness according to the size of the lecture theater or classroom and to the acoustical properties of the particular location. In very large lecture halls it may be necessary for the professor occasionally to inquire whether those in the farthest section can hear and understand.

Not only should the instructor be concerned about the loudness of the voice to assure that all of the members of the class can catch what is being said, but volume, like rate and inflection, must also be utilized to harmonize with different moods and attitudes, and should vary from loud to soft in conveying various meanings.

Quality Change

Voice quality comprises such voice characteristics as voice timbre and color and is largely determined by the shape and size of the resonating chambers — the open throat, mouth, sinuses (cheek bones and forehead) and nasal cavities, as well as the length of the vocal chords. Correct resonation affects voice quality. When we speak of someone having a pleasant-sounding voice, we are generally referring to voice quality. Voice quality is also definitely related to the individual's personality. Even though the general quality of the voice should be resonant, there must be variations from good quality to harshness to express such attitudes as indignation or determination, or even at times anger or irony.

It is suprising how the human voice is capable of portraying a very wide range of mental attitudes, feelings and moods through a manipulation of these four aspects of vocal variety. Once again we must remember that the purpose of using vocal variety is to communicate, not to distract or obstruct communication. The use of all of the various types of vocal variety — in other words *how* the teacher speaks — should be consistent with the personality and be appropriate to the ideas being expressed and to the specific teaching situation. Above all, these changes in the voice for the purpose of conveying meaning should be natural and spontaneous. This is summed up in the book, *The Teacher Speaks* in the following words:

> These four speech elements — voice quality, pitch, time, and loudness — integrate in effective speech regardless of the occasion. If any one of these elements is held constant, monotonous speech results. And there is nothing more deadly and deadening than monotony. A single quality of voice, a constant rate of speech, a monopitch . . . a repeated rhythm throughout a talk, or a single degree of loudness takes from the speech. . . . If two or more of the elements fail to be flexible and varied, the quality of the speech drops far below the desired level for teachers.
>
> It is through the flexibility of speech that we say what we mean in a manner that will interest our hearers. . . . Teachers must not only speak; they must speak well. In wide-awake, intelligent speech there is a constant shift within and among the speech elements. A good speaker must learn to control these changes.[11]

The *verbal* and the *vocal* messages should both be in harmony with each other. The actual words themselves should not convey to the listeners one thought, while the vocal variety in the voice is portraying something else, or even indicating an opposite meaning, except, of course, for the purpose of creating an effect, as in the use of irony or sarcasm.

NONVERBAL COMMUNICATION

The words used by the teacher and also the way in which these words are spoken constitute the verbal aspects of delivery, and we have noted some of the ways in which communication may break down in these areas. Now let us turn our attention to the various nonverbal aspects of delivery, and we will see how the nonuse or the incorrect use of the body can greatly decrease the teacher's effectiveness. The visible portion of "speaking" is very important to classroom communication. We have often heard it said that "actions speak louder than words." The stimuli that enter the mind via the avenue of the eyes produce a much more indelible impression than that which reaches the brain through the other senses of perception.

Bodily Movement

From the very moment the instructor enters the classroom at the beginning of the lecture or class period, until the students leave at the close of the class, the teacher's body is communicating messages and in some way influencing the members of the course by physical appearance and visible actions. The clothes, hair style, general appearance and demeanor constitute a potential influence on the students. Dress and appearance, like the voice, should not unduly call attention to themselves so as to detract from the verbal message. These external concerns should fit the personality of the teacher, and unless hampered by an attitude of conformity, these are expressions of the teacher's personality.

More important than these, however, is the conscious and unconscious (spontaneous) use of the body in the process of communicating the subject materials. As Sarett and Foster pointed out, bodily movements are necessary to the effective transmission of ideas and concepts: "No speaker can reach his maximum effectiveness — indeed, in many cases he cannot hope to reach even moderate effectiveness — unless he understands thoroughly the uses of bodily action."[12] Correct bodily movements should be spontaneous, natural, and unnoticable, but they should be meaningful, becoming an intricate part of the overall communication process. Awkward bodily movements which are ill timed, inappropriate, or too repetitious can constitute barriers to communication, because they interfere with the free flow of ideas from speaker to listener and detract from what is being said. They may not only annoy, but actually confuse the students, because these movements can send out an entirely different set of signals than those being conveyed by the verbal and vocal stimuli.

Correct Posture

Body actions include gestures of the hands, arms and shoulders, facial expressions, eye contact and also posture. Posture is a matter of attitude. The teacher should stand tall and erect, but not rigid or tense. The hands should remain in a relaxed position at the teacher's sides when not employed in gestures. They should not be in pockets or clenching the speaker's desk. Many teachers remain seated while lecturing and more often during discussions. There are, however, some psychological advantages to standing, and certainly this is true for the lecture method of teaching. Some professors walk around while lecturing or sit on the edge of the desk (or even on the desk with their legs and feet dangling), and occasionally these actions are permissible, but if done to excess they, like so many other things during delivery, can detract from the prime purpose of conveying intellectual ideas to the students.

Good Eye Contact

"Seeing is believing." If the students can see the professor as enthusiastic and earnest about what he is saying, and if before them day after day they can witness expressions of genuine feelings of concern for their intellectual development, these attitudes along with the subject matter will be conveyed more readily. If, however, the professor's vocal utterances are lifeless and facial expressions are somber and dull, classroom communication will surely suffer.

Not only can the eyes be very expressive, but the eyes assure a point of contact between teacher and student. If the students are looking elsewhere than at the instructor, it can be safely assumed that their minds are not making contact with the words being spoken. Whenever the teacher takes his eyes off the students and looks elsewhere, whether it be on the manuscript or at the floor or ceiling etc., communication is broken or, at least greatly reduced. Long quotations should be avoided, but when it becomes necessary to use them the teacher should look up at the students sometime during every few sentences. As mentioned earlier, good eye contact is one of the greatest advantages of extemporaneous teaching over manuscript reading.

Meaningful Gestures

Cicero considered gestures to be more powerful than words. If the teacher is too inhibited to use gestures, or if the gestures are inappropriate, much will be lost in the process of transmitting information and ideas to the students. Gestures may be classified into three groups: (1) emphatic — clenched fist or tenseness of arms and hands, to portray seriousness and determination; (2) descriptive — motions indicating shape, size and direction; and (3) suggestive — pointing, shrugging of shoulders, etc.

The same principles that apply to vocal and facial expressions are likewise true of the use of gestures, namely, they should be motivated, meaningful, natural, and spontaneous, not calling attention to themselves. They must be communicative without being conspicuous. The type and intensity of gestures used in a lecture and other teaching methods, should not be incongruent to either the personality of the professor or to the degree of formality of the teaching situation (such as in very large lecture halls where prominent and sweeping gestures might be more appropriate than in the small seminar room). Gestures serve the purpose of relieving nervous tension of the teacher (especially beginning instructors), of holding the attention of the students (activity and movement as factors of attention), and of reinforcing and enhancing meaning to the words that are spoken and the concepts and ideas being expressed.

Repetition of any kind, whether it be of facial or body gestures, calls attention to itself after the third or fourth time in relatively close proximity. Gestures should be varied, lest they become a form of mannerism, and the students look for these to reappear (and later mimic them).

Concerning the relationship between gestures to personal effectiveness in teaching, Fessenden, Johnson, and Larson wrote:

> You will need to keep in mind Hamlet's advice to the players, "suit the action to the word, and the word to the action." You cannot say one thing with your body and another with your voice and your words. . .
>
> The longer you work on it, the more you will integrate and coordinate your words and actions. The more you bring voice and body into unity of purpose and behavior the greater will be your personal effectiveness.[13]

Perhaps there are those who are not willing to work hard at learning how to use normal bodily actions to convey emotions and attitudes, or are so inhibited and reluctant to develop rapport with their students, so what is perfectly natural in conversational speaking seems to them ridiculous in a more formal setting. Perhaps this is why McLeish referred to facial expressions and gestures as "facial grimaces" and "bodily contortions and extreme motor activity which some popular exponents of the lecture find invaluable in holding the attention of their audiences."[14] It is much easier to criticize the lecture method (or any aspect of college and university teaching) than to rise above mediocrity in performance. It does take a lot of hard work, but as Edward Sheffield observed, it is this hard work that distinguishes, more than anything else, the effective teachers from the ineffective ones. These are the ones who are dedicated and conscientious and who are demanding of themselves as well as their students, because they work hard at class preparation and presentation.

PRONUNCIATION

Articulation relates to speaking in such a way (with flexible articulators) that every syllable of each word can be clearly and distinctly understood. Articulation that is overprecise will call attention to itself, and words that are slurred or mumbled cannot be instantaneously understood, and in either extreme, communication suffers. Articulation and enunciation refers to clarity in expressing the vowels and consonants. Many teachers are guilty of sloppy articulation due to inflexible articulators, or as Dr. Alan Monroe in my graduate classes at Purdue used to say, poor articulation was the result of "lazy lips and an idle tongue." Here is another area where every teacher could exert some of the *hard work* in an effort to correct or perfect delivery.

Pronunciation relates to correctness, whereas articulation concerns itself with clarity. An individual might articulate clearly, but at the same time mispronounce words. On the other hand, he might pronounce his word correctly but fail to make his voice and words clearly discernible. Any departure from the accepted pronunciation hinders the process of communication and becomes a barrier. As mentioned before, the mass media has made the average person, not only voice conscious but also language conscious. What constitutes good pronunciation? By consulting the dictionary and by observing the speech of the educated people in the area, one can determine what is the correct pronunciation. Years ago, W.H. Broadie, Head of Broadcast Language with CBC in Canada, recognizing the importance of good pronunciation in any speaking situation, gave this advice to announcers:

> Perhaps the most unforgivable fault is carelessness or slovenliness of speech. The mispronunciation of English words, the use of ungrammatical or illiterate speech, are as reprehensible as to appear at a dinner party with dirty fingernails and soiled linen. Ignorance is no excuse, for the means of curing ignorance are always at hand; the neglect to consult a dictionary when in doubt is an insult to the listener. Moreover, in this respect the announcer must remember that his speech is listened to by many who consciously or unconsciously take him for a model; his responsibility then is great, and he must be correspondingly careful to exercise it properly. [15]

Good pronunciation is not showy. The best pronunciation attracts the least attention to itself. If students say, "What a beautiful voice he has, and what precise language he uses," the teacher has distracted their attention to the voice and words, instead of to the message. The best pronunciation is clear but inconspicuous. Good pronunication is not overprecise. Overniceness of pronunciation is as much to be avoided as carelessness. Labored precision is an offense to good taste. The best pronunciation is that which is easy and natural and relatively free from local or regional accent. Concerning this, Ehninger et al. wrote:

> Unfortunately, dialects and regional pronunciations may produce not only misunderstanding between speakers and listeners, but often they may also produce *negative judgments* — judgments which may seriously affect some auditors' perceptions of the speaker's credibility, education, reliability, responsibility, and capabilities for leadership. [16]

In my classes in voice and diction, I call to the attention of the students twenty different faults of pronunciation. Some of the most common ones are listed below:

1. Misplaced accents — "genu-íne," "de-vice," "the-áy-ter."
2. Omission of sounds — "guvment" for government; "particuly" for particularly; "innernational," for international.
3. Additions of sounds, — "athalete."
4. Substitution of sounds, especially the "d" for the "t" in the final position in polysyllabic words like "communidy," "humididy," "sociedy," and in the case of the medial double t's as in "budder" for butter; "liddle" for little; and "ladder" for latter. (Each time I return to America from England, I become more aware of the

extent to which many mispronounce words in this "partikilar,"
I mean particular aspect!)

5. Transposition of sounds — "pernounce" for pronounce; "inner-
   duce" or "interduce" for introduce (substitution and transposition of sounds).
6. Confusing similar-sounding words as partition and petition.
7. Carelessness — "jist," "git" and "becuz," for just, get and because.

Other reasons for faulty pronunciation come under the classification of foreign influence or regional dialect, substandard speech or
degradation, incorrect assimilation, and plain ignorance. Not only
do these faults constitute barriers to classroom communication, but
anyone, especially one engaged in some form of public speaking, is
categorized socially, culturally and intellectually by the way he pro-
nounces (or mispronounces) words.

VOICE TRAINING NECESSARY FOR COLLEGE
AND UNIVERSITY TEACHERS

Arthur Wise, in his chapter "Talking to Large Groups," referred
to a study conducted by the speech staff of the University of Leeds
Department of Education. This study, involving the graduate teachers in training, revealed that one-third of them had "speech that was
in some way unsatisfactory for classroom communication purposes."
In an effort to locate the cause for this alarming situation, Wise
stated:

> Since there is no Speech Education process that a lecturer has been
> subjected to, he must depend almost entirely on personal background
> and what may have been gleaned from experience. . . . So, although
> some university teachers have considerable skill in handling such a com-
> plicated speech situation as the lecture, we cannot assume that this will
> necessarily be so in every case. There is no reason to suppose that the
> new university teacher will be any more competent in lecturing than
> would be the butcher, the baker or the candlestick maker. We can only
> guarantee lecturing competence by some deliberate educational inter-
> vention, some process that sets out to develop the speech skill of a person
> who will spend much of his professional life trying to impart information
> and attitudes in oral terms.[17]

According to the *Report of Commission on Teaching in Higher Education*, presented to Liverpool Conference, April, 1969, students in British colleges and universities feel strongly about the apparent lack of training in lecturing evidenced in their classes. Even though some argue that students are not competent to judge the merit of either the process or the results of teaching and are often immature, superficial, mistaken and prejudiced, the learner's attitudes cannot be ignored. These attitudes are important to the educational process. Students are in a position to observe the teaching process day after day, and student opinion may direct attention to attitudes, methods of instruction and teacher personality that are undesirable, and of which the teacher and administrators may not be aware.

Much of the previously mentioned report was based on questionnaires sent to college and university students. On the last page of the questionnaire the respondents were asked for further comments concerning the abilities of lecturers. From the considerable volume of responses in this section and from such earlier specific questions such as, "Do you feel that lecturers should receive training in the basic art of lecturing?" many comments were received which seemed to indicate that these were not "purely spontaneous or unthinking responses." The good lecturers received praise and even "reverence," but "there was extremely heavy criticism of many others."

> There was an annoyed despair and an attitude of inevitability about many of these cases, but the general feeling was undoubtedly that the overall standard of lecturing was below what it should be. The point was not made truculently or insultingly and certainly not unconstructively, but was reasoned and emphatic if only by virtue of its constant repetition. . . . Students in colleges of education found it heavily ironic that a lecturer in education and teaching methods should himself be incapable of communicating effectively. . . . The universities were undoubtedly the most profuse in their criticism. . . . The desirability of lecture training was particularly apparent here in whatever subject, and the point was once raised that lecturers once employed should be inspected periodically as were school-teachers.[18]

Many complained that current lecture courses were frequently superfluous. For those who were training to become teachers there was a desire for more teaching practice and more instruction in basic teaching methods. This plea for lecture training was reinforced by logic, namely, "that academic qualifications are valueless if the knowledge cannot be imparted to others at a later date." Students considered it unfortunate that lecturers were hired for their research potential rather than their lecturing ability. Furthermore, it appeared as though promotion was determined by the research and publishing achievements rather than on any apparent extent of competence in the lecture-theater.

This commission, in cooperation with other concerned groups, felt that some financial incentive in terms of grants for a lecturer wishing to be trained would be a start in the right direction. This would provide the untrained teacher with some measure of professional training in lecturing, but this could not be regarded as a substitute for a course of professional training. In one year alone (1967 — 68) there were approximately 1,000 new entrants to the profession, and it would take many specialized courses to train those just entering the teaching profession at this level.

> The present arrangement basically discourages a lecturer from training until he is already well-entrenched in his profession. Without wishing to decry in-service training, this does mean that, rather than arriving already trained, a new lecturer is gaining his teaching experience at the expense of students who have a mere three years to gain their most vital qualifications. It is unfortunate if the successful completion of this task is in any way jeopardized by their being taught by individuals totally unqualified to teach.[19]

One of the recommendations of this commission was that all lecturers at institutions of higher and further education should be trained in how to lecture, preferably before taking up their positions, and where this is not possible they should receive some training during the first three years of their appointment.

The commission recognized that "lecturing is a science, not an acquired taste; as such it can be transmitted, learnt and improved upon." The salary scales for lecturers should be determined according to their training in lecturing skills and teaching qualifications. The commission made the following recommendation:

> That the salary scales for lecturers should be adjusted so as to make greater allowances for the possession of teaching qualifications. In the long-term, we consider that the salary "norm" should be that paid to a lecturer with teaching qualifications and that unqualified lecturers be paid below this norm.[20]

The teacher's delivery should always be a means to an end. All of the various components of delivery such as bodily action — gestures, posture, facial expression, eye contact; vocal flexibility — rate, volume (projection), inflection, voice quality; and diction — articulation, enunciation, pronunciation; all play their part in the teacher's total responsibility of communicating knowledge, attitudes and inspiration to the students. Defects, distortions or inadequacies in any of these aspects of the teacher's delivery will give occasion for partial hindrance or total obstruction in classroom communication.

NOTES

1. Eble, Kenneth E.: *The Craft of Teaching*. San Francisco, Jossey-Bass Pub., 1976, p. 44.
2. Schwartz, Lita Lizer: Criteria for effective university teaching, *Improving College and University Teaching, 28, No. 3*:120, Summer, 1980.
3. Schwartz, Lita Lizer: Criteria for effective university teaching. p. 120.
4. Rovin, Sheldon, Lalonde, Ernest, and Haley, John H.: An assessment of the lecture. *Improving College and University Teaching, 20*:326, 327, Autumn, 1972.
5. Wise, Arthur: Talking to large groups. In Layton, David (Ed.): *University Teaching in Transition*. Edinburgh, Oliver and Boyd, 1968, p. 38.
6. Quintilian: *The Institution Oratoria of Quintilian*, xi, iii, trans. Butler, H.E. New York, G.P. Putnam's Sons, 1922, p. 245.
7. Thonssen, Lester, and Baird, A. Craig: *Speech Criticism*. New York, Ronald Press, 1948, p. 446.
8. Ehninger, Douglas, Monroe, Alan H., and Gronbeck, Bruce E.: *Principles and Types of Speech Communication*, 8th ed. Glenview, Scott, Foresman and Co., 1978, p. 412.
9. Beard, R.M., Bligh, D.A., and Harding, A.G.: *Research into Teaching Methods in Higher Education*, 4th ed. Guildford, Society for Research in Higher Education, 1978, p. 40.
10. Fessenden, Seth A., Johnson, Roy Ivan, and Larson, P. Merville: *The Teacher Speaks*. New York, Prentice-Hall, Inc., 1954, p. 84.
11. Fessenden, Seth A., Johnson, Roy Ivan, and Larson, P. Merville: *The Teacher Speaks*. p. 87.
12. Sarett, Lew, and Foster, William Trufant: *Basic Principles of Speech*. Boston, Houghton Mifflin Co., 1936, p. 128.
13. Fessenden, et. al.: *The Teacher Speaks*. p. 65.
14. McLeish, John: *The Lecture Method*. Cambridge, Cambridge Institute of Education, 1968, Heffers of Cambridge, Printers, p. 5.
15. French, Florence: *Radio English*. New York, McGraw-Hill, 1952, pp. 114, 115.

16. Ehninger, Douglas, *et al.*: *Principles and Types of Speech Communication.* pp. 243, 244.
17. Wise, Arthur: Talking to large groups. pp. 35, 36.
18. *Report of Commission on Teaching in Higher Education,* presented to Liverpool Conference, April, 1969. London, National Union of Students, 1969, pp. 38, 39.
19. *Report of Commission on Teaching in Higher Education.* p. 51.
20. *Report of Commission on Teaching in Higher Education.* p. 55.

CHAPTER 8

AVOIDING LANGUAGE BARRIERS

I recognize but one mental acquisition as an essential part
of the education of a lady or gentleman, namely an accurate
and refined use of the mother tongue.
Charles W. Eliot

The essence of the lecture is the spoken word.
I.A. Richards

SINCE the use of language, especially the oral aspect of language, plays such an important part in education, both from the standpoint of the teacher and student, it would be well to review some of the potential semantic barriers to communication. The last chapter stressed the importance of voice and bodily actions. The emphasis was on the techniques of communication — *how* to speak. In this chapter more emphasis will be placed upon the substance or content of communication — *what* to say, although when we consider the use of language, we are not thinking so much of what thoughts and ideas to express, as the kind of language with which to clothe our concepts. Words are the main vehicle of our classroom communication. Words can also become sources of hindrance to communication. Language has been defined as a system of predetermined symbols understood by the communicator and the listener or observer.

COMMUNICATION BARRIERS IN LANGUAGE

Because of the nature and limitations of language itself and the frailties of the human mind, there never can be 100 percent communication between two or more individuals. Perfect communication is only possible theoretically. There are at least a dozen areas in the use of language as a form of communication where potential barriers or pitfalls exist, some (or all) of which occur during every class period of instruction. For the purpose of preciseness and clarity, the main language communication barriers will be enumerated and briefly explained.

1. The first linguistic barrier to be recognized in teaching is the fact that no one person can possibly know all there is to know about any single object or concept. Since one does not or cannot comprehend anything completely, one cannot, consequently, convey to others what cannot be fully understood.

2. Even the things that an individual does grasp mentally and feels emotionally, cannot be perfectly or even adequately represented by word symbols. In other words, a person's own experiences in life and perceptions about life cannot be suitably translated into language to his own complete satisfaction, much less that of others. Not only is it impossible for us to perceive every detail of any given object or concept, but the fact remains that no amount of word symbols can possibly represent all of the aspects of reality that we are able to receive with our senses.

3. Even if a person could know everything about an object or concept, and even if he could find the exact words which could fully and accurately convey the precise meaning of all that he understood, it would be impossible for him to evoke in the mind of the one with whom he is communicating, the same image that he has in his own mind. In the first place, the listener might not be able to comprehend all of what the speaker understands and which he endeavors to communicate to the hearer, and in the second place, each word symbol has a slightly (or vastly) different meaning to each person involved in the communication situation.

Words have different emotive associations to each individual person, because everyone has had a different experience or experiences attached to the referent of the word. Every teacher's own background, experience and personality definitely influences the word meaning for himself or herself. Concerning this phenomenon Rudolf Flesch wrote:

> In one way or another, your language differs from that of anybody else. It's part of your own unique personality. It has traces of the family you grew up in, the place where you came from, the people you have associated with, the jobs you have had, the schools you went to, the books you have read, your hobbies, your sports, your philosophy, your religion, your politics, your prejudices, your memories, your ambitions, your dreams, and your love life. The way you form your sentences shows your outlook on life: the words you choose show your temperament and your aspirations.[1]

The first essential in the determination of the meaning of a word is the definition of its referent. The referent is the particular action, object or the relation between the actions or objects, or their characteristics for which the word stands. The referent, then is the thing to which the symbol refers. Instead of reality, it is our subjective perception of reality. The same symbol may have different subjective perceptions, and, as mentioned, our subjective perception is never complete. No two individuals ever have exactly the same referent. A word is merely a substitute stimulus or response, and its meaning depends on what particular experiences have been associated with it. The word itself is meaningless, but when it stands for some thing, object, action, etc., then it takes on meaning.

The letters *x* or *y* are meaningless in themselves, but the mathematician can make each stand for a certain proposition or problem. Instead of repeating the entire proposition or problem each time he refers to them, he simply uses the symbols *x* and *y*. Words, likewise, abbreviate the processes of thought and analyzing of details. When we refer to a tree, we mean the leaves, branches, trunk, bark, etc. The real meaning of an object is our attitude toward that object, and our reaction to it.

Not only is the teacher in the communication process confronted with this *partial* breakdown of communication, due to the fact that words mean different things to different people, but worse than this, there may be *complete* blockage of communication if the words, concepts, or ideas may mean a certain thing to the teacher because of past experiences and associations with the word symbol, but which have *no* meaning at all to the listener. Try defining and describing a gorgeous sunrise or sunset to a person who has never had sight. What meaning would the expression *white as snow* have to the African desert dweller who has never seen snow, not even on a distant mountain peak?

4. To further complicate the potential language barrier, meaning may vary for a given word within the same person, depending on some new emotional experience he or she may have had which is now associated with that expression or symbol. The words *home* and *family* may have had one connotative meaning at one time in the life of a person, but because of continual emotional disturbances or divorce, these words may mean something completely different.

The same word referring to the same physical object may have completely different emotive meanings to the same individual at different times and under different circumstances. The word *snow* has a completely different meaning to a person after struggling with hazardous driving conditions during several severe winters in Michigan than it does when drinking in the breathtaking beauties of the Matterhorn on a midsummer holiday. The word *snow* evokes pleasant feelings to a child, especially if it rarely falls in the area in which he resides, but changes its meaning when, as a crippled old man he is forced to remain indoors all winter because of the heavy snow in the locality of his retirement.

5. Since the meaning of words rests in people and not in the word itself, language is constantly in a state of flux. The change may take place very gradually until it can, in fact, have the exact opposite meaning in some cases, but at least a slightly or completely different meaning. I remember the reaction of the students in my class a few years ago, when I used such words as *trip* and *gay* in their former connotations. In everyday language the meanings of words are constantly shifting, especially in the expressions employed by students. I have even noted some language understanding gaps between the younger children and the older children in my own family. Aside from the teen-age jargon, the meaning of many of the words in our language gradually shifts during the normal

lifetime of an individual. Smith today is not the same Smith tomorrow, or of ten years ago, nor ten years from now. Heraclitus said, "You can not step into the same river twice." The symbols with which we do our thinking remain fixed, but their referents are constantly changing. Therefore, the meanings often become blurred, and there is a lack of correspondence between the word and the reality.

6. Not only do words not mean the same thing to everyone, or change in meaning, but they constitute a further communication breakdown when there is vagueness and ambiguity. This results in confusion because there is no real or definite concept of meaning attached to that word. It is difficult to isolate single and unmistakable meanings from certain nebulous labels and slogans. Ullmann gives four reasons for vagueness and ambiguity:

1. Generic character of the words — refer to classes rather than specifics,
2. Multiplicity of aspects — depending on the context, situation, and personality of the speaker etc.,
3. Lack of clear cut edges — example, color spectrum,
4. Lack of familiarity with referents — highly variable depending on knowledge and interests of the individual.[2]

Irving Lee illustrated how a word or label like *the American way* is ambiguous, and how even the vagueness associated with this expression has changed in meaning:

> We are prone to wax eloquent over "the American way," without reflecting that there have been many changes in the American mode of living since the founding of the nation, and that there may have been certain phases in that mode which have not been wholly admirable. Similarly, we continue to speak of "communism" without considering the possibility that . . . (it) is somewhat different from the communism of 1918.[3]

Salomon suggested four ways of curbing the dangers of ambiguous words and phrases: (1) by pointing out examples, (2) by giving synonyms for the word, (3) by reference to larger categories with indication of particulars, and (4) by describing the word in terms of the operations to be performed or at least capable in principle of being performed in order to translate the concept into perceptual terms.[4]

7. Every discipline and every profession has its specialized terms and jargon. The teacher must be careful not to assume that the students will understand these words. Every specialized term or expression peculiar to the subject matter must be fully explained as these words and expressions appear in the lecture or discussion.

8. Another area of language that could produce a communication breakdown relates to the fact that at times teachers use an abstract word symbol in reference to a quality or thing, which has either a *symbolic* or relative meaning which may not be accepted or understood at the moment of utterance. In language, we group things into certain classes. This classification depends on the similar or common characteristics, and ignore parts that do not agree. We say that a dog is an animal, and a horse is an animal, implying that there are certain common characteristics, but recognizing certain differences. We might state that the neighbor is a mule, by which we mean that we have observed that the neighbor had at least one quality — stubbornness, which we presume is an observed quality or characteristic attribute of the animal we refer to as a mule. The higher the order of abstraction the more difficult it becomes to determine the specific referent for the symbol, and the higher the level of abstraction the more vague is this referenct.

9. The teacher should be aware of yet another common form of language communication breakdown, which results from the assumption or implication that all things in a given category are included in a simple statement about them. *Allness* is an overgeneralizing from one example to the extention of all other like things in the same general classification. This often leads to prejudice in reference to sex, race, religions, cultures and ethnic groups. Everything within a grouping or category is classified as having the same characteristics, and there is no provision made for individual differences in details. Irving Lee refers to *allness* as a disease of details being left out. This problem of universal application is partially due to our desire to define terms, when we say that a thing *is* such and such. In commenting on definitions, Irving Lee stated that "when a

form of the verb 'to be' connects a noun and an adjective we invariably express false-to-fact relationship."[5]

10. The teacher must be aware of words that have double meanings or connotations and subtle suggestions that can be interpreted by the students as either intentional or unintentional propaganda or prejudice. Words, as symbols can arouse the preexisting attitudes that are at the basis of all suggestion, and in this way language becomes the chief medium through which propaganda operates. Concerning the differences between the intentional and unintentional propaganda and the way words and language influence the thinking and attitudes as well as the behavior of the listener toward goals which are unethical, Doob wrote:

> Intentional propaganda is a systematic attempt by an interested individual (or individuals) to control the attitudes of groups of individuals through the use of suggestion and, consequently, to control their actions; unintentional propaganda is the control of the attitudes and, consequently, the actions of groups of individuals through the use of suggestion. In intentional propaganda, the propagandist is aware of his interested aim; in unintentional propaganda, he does not appreciate the social effect of his own actions.[6]

In listing the three attributes of most words, Doob quoted Erdmann. "The conceptual content, which is more or less definite, the secondary meaning, and the feeling tone. . . . The secondary meaning of a word and the 'feeling' attached thereto are other ways of describing the pre-existing attitudes aroused by a symbol."[7]

Hayakawa succinctly differentiates between denotative and connotative meanings of words according to their *extensional* and *intentional* usages.

> Denotative and extensional are terms we use to indicate the "point" quality of a word. With these we designate the object, concept, quality or action. Connotative and intensional designate personal associations that have gathered around a word.[8]

It is crucial that the teacher remain sensitive not only to the denotative but also the connotative meaning of words and expressions.

STRUCTURAL MEANING

Another aspect or dimension of meaning and language usage with which the teacher should obviously be cognizant is the structural meaning. In order to construct sentences effectively, we need some procedures for arranging words in sequences. The term grammar has, perhaps, some of the unpleasant connotative meaning to which I have just been alluding. It is superfluous to state the importance for the college and university professors to avoid falling into the many snares of ungrammatical or illiterate speech. Sloppy articulation, mispronunciation, and awkward sentence structure as well as grammatical errors do not automatically vanish when a professor is granted a doctoral degree! This is not the place to review all of the rules for correct grammar, but in passing, I will allude briefly to only two of the most notorious and appalling grammatical errors — the use of a singular *to be* verb followed by a plural object, or the common use of the plural pronoun and verb following *everyone* or *one* and *each* as in, "Each one occupying the seats in this classroom *have their. . . .*" instead of "has his. . . ." Any of the previously mentioned errors in the use of the English language is a disgrace to the profession and an insult to the recipients. The professor's lecture (or utterances in any teaching situation) ought to be an example of cultured speech.

VOCABULARY

The teacher needs to select the words with the exact shades of meaning. A restricted or very limited vocabulary could become a major barrier to classroom communication. The teacher must work diligently to choose words that are accurate, clear, appropriate, and vivid. Concerning correctness in word choice, Thonssen, Baird, and Braden stated:

> The virtue of correctness thus embraces a variety of concepts, including those of words and of their union. . . . It deals with word choice that insures accuracy in developing the speaker's thought an accuracy that is unimpaired by modish colloquialisms, archaisms, and word coinages. Correctness facilitates the use of language as an effective vehicle for conveying thought.[9]

Our vocabulary at the comprehension level is much greater than at the vocal level. In acquiring a large vocabulary, I am not suggesting that the teacher memorize difficult-sounding words and phrases to parade before the students, who may for the moment be impressed with such knowledge and ability. Good vocabulary means the effective use of simple words. The English are noted for verbal flexibility and the use of picturesque language to a far greater extent than generally found among Americans. They are much more apt to employ strong nouns, active verbs and descriptive adjectives and adverbs. For example, instead of saying, "the man *fixed* the flat tire;" "the woman *fixed* the table;" and "the florist *fixed* the bouquet of flowers," the English would probably substitute such words as *repaired* the tire (tyre), *set* the table, and *arranged* the bouquet.

If the vocabulary, word choice and sentence structure are so plain or limited that they fail to draw mental images in the minds of the listener, or if the expressions are so trite that they have lost their charm or meaning, communication has been adversely effected. On the other hand, if the style is so embellished and ornate that the hearer is carried away with the language, attention is distracted from *what* is being said to *how* it is being spoken, and again communication suffers. The highest ends can be reached by the simplest means, and this is a great secret in the use of words.

To acquire such a command of the language, the teacher must read widely, attempt to add to his vocabulary by trying out new words and expressions frequently, and actively using the full range of the vocabulary already acquired. As mentioned, each individual has several *kinds* of vocabularies. The largest one consists of the words he recognizes, especially in context, as they are heard, spoken or seen in print. Another vocabulary is the one he uses in writing, and finally the oral vocabulary. Most people are acquainted with the meaning of ten times as many words as they actually use in speaking. The effective teacher will try to transfer as many words from his *recognition* vocabulary to his *active* vocabulary, not for display, but for the sole utilitarian purpose of communicating vividly and precisely the meaning of ideas and concepts.

Style

"Style is excellent when, like the atmosphere, it shows the thought, but itself is not seen."[10] Good language style is a tremendous aid in communication because it holds the attenton of the listener, by firing his imagination with vivid word pictures, revealing the unknown through analogies, quickens the understanding and stirs the mind into action. On the other hand, a lack of style wearies the listener with boredom, because it is devoid of variations and becomes insipid, flat and colorless. Dullness of style is primarily the result of dull minds, dull lives and unimaginative personalities. President Eliot of Harvard said, "It is a liberal education which teaches a man to speak and write his native language strongly, accurately, and persuasively. It is a sufficient reward for the whole long course of twelve years spent in liberal study."[11]

Sentence structure, which is a part of style, refers to the length of sentences, the smoothness or awkwardness of expression and of sentence variety. In an oral style sentences should be relatively simple in construction and brief, although to break the monotony, an occasional compound, complex sentence can be interjected. At times the sentences should be inverted. It is much more important for an oral style to have a balance of different kinds of sentence structure. No pattern should be discernible, lest this recurring arrangement attract attention to itself and detract from the subject matter being presented.

Rhetorical devices such as figures of speech will help to brighten up a prosaic, unimaginative lecture. According to Wilson and Arnold:

> Figures of speech are forms of expression which serve to intensify meanings. They make their points indirectly by stating things vividly in terms of something else. They are not literally meant or interpreted. They enhance ideas by making them more graphic and appealing. Like all comparisons, contrasts, and exemplifications, figures of speech are especially useful in translating the unknown into terms of the known.[12]

Arthur E. Phillips, in his book *Effective Speaking*, a favorite of public speakers, clearly enunciated the importance and principles of the efficacious use of language.

> To be most effective in our choice of words three things are essential.

We must be intelligible, we must be intelligible adequately, that is, we must be understood by the persons addressed, in the sense and degree we desire, and further, we must be adquately intelligible in the briefest time. To achieve these ends, we must develop the power of ready and varied verbal expression.[13]

Imagery can be used to stimulate all of the senses by recalling images which the hearers have previously experienced. The listeners can thus re-create an image of a person, place, object or idea in their minds and associate attitudes, feelings or values with the words they hear. Concerning the use of imagery, Wilson and Arnold wrote:

While we may customarily think of imagery as a poetic device, it can also be employed by oral communicators to fill out details and to arouse or engage the feelings of audiences — an engagement which, in turn, provides bases for positive or negative attitudinal and valuative judgments.[14]

If language is employed merely for the purpose of display, or consciously restricted for fear of embellishment, or if it is simply *natively* poor for lack of intelligence, interest, or effort, communication in the classroom will suffer.

Whether we view education from the point of view of its social objectives, or more narrowly, from the point of view of personal and individual development, language becomes the indispensable vehicle of learning, the means by which and through which educational progress is accelerated and our educational goals attained.[15]

McFarland pointed out how important language is to every aspect of teaching and learning and that the teacher has a definite responsibility to the students in using language wisely.

Language has so many functions — communicating and eliciting information and explanations, expressing and exploring problems, expressing personal attitudes or cultural assumptions, inviting or excluding the participation of others, elaborating trains of logical reasoning, or venting emotions, affirming and questioning, raising and dashing hopes, evoking pride and shame. Teachers, like others, slip in and out of these various uses of language, leaving behind them a trail of human effects that may be intentional or unintentional, and (in either case) admirable or disastrous.[16]

NOTES

1. Flesch, Rudolf: *The Art of Readable Writing.* New York, Harper and Brothers, 1949, p. 205.
2. Ullmann, Stephen: Words with blurred edges. In Anderson, Wallace L., and Stageberg, Norman C. (Eds.): *Introductory Readings in Language.* (Rev. ed.) New York, Holt, Rinehart, and Winston, 1966, pp. 126-132.
3. Lee, Irving J.: *Language Habits in Human Affairs.* New York, Harper and Brothers, 1941, p. 78.
4. Salomon, Louis B.: *Semantics and Common Sense.* New York, Holt, Rinehart, and Winston, Inc., 1966, p. 55.
5. Lee, Irving J.: *Language Habits in Human Affairs.* p. 243.
6. Doob, Leonard W.: *Propaganda.* New York, Henry Holt and Co., 1935, p. 89.
7. Doob, Leonard W.: *Propaganda.* p. 60, quoting Erdmann.
8. Hayakawa, S.I.: *Language in Thought and Action.* London, George Allen and Unwin, Ltd., 1952, p. 58.
9. Thonssen, Lester, Baird, A. Craig, and Braden, Waldo W.: *Speech Criticism*, 2nd ed. New York, The Ronald Press, 1970, p. 489.
10. Thonssen, Lester, et.al.: *Speech Criticism.* p. 498, quoting Philo Buck and John Broadus.
11. Jefferson, Charles Edward: *The Minister as Prophet.* New York, Gosset and Dunlap. 1905, pp. 117, 118, quoting Charles Eliot.
12. Wilson, John F., and Arnold, Carroll C.: *Public Speaking as a Liberal Art.* 2nd ed. Boston, Allyn and Bacon, Inc., 1968, p. 303.
13. Phillips, Arthur E.: *Effective Speaking.* Chicago, The Newton Co., 1938, p. 70.
14. Wilson and Arnold: *Public Speaking as a Liberal Art.* p. 293.
15. Fessenden, Seth A., Johnson, Roy Ivan, and Larson, P. Merville: *The Teacher Speaks.* New York, Prentice-Hall, Inc., 1954, p. 7.
16. McFarland, Henry Steward Noel: *Intelligent Teaching.* London, Routledge and Kegan Paul, 1973, p. 73.

CHAPTER 9

LECTURES THAT MOTIVATE STUDENTS

There is little doubt that student motivation is an important factor affecting the performance of students in their courses. Indeed, there is some evidence that it is more important than intelligence.
Bligh

THUS far the various ways have been considered in which communication from the teacher to the student can break down or interfere with the learning process. The teacher may not be knowledgeable in the subject area, in which case he cannot share something with others that he himself does not possess. It may be that the teacher is disinterested in either the subject or the students, or both, or possesses traits of personality that repel the students and cause them to "turn a deaf ear" to what is being said. Classroom communication may break down because of one or many of the faults in the transmission of the knowledge, through lack of organization, lack of attention and interest, wrong teaching method or poor delivery and ineffective use of language.

In this chapter attention will be drawn to a major barrier to classroom communication which occurs *after* the knowledge has been received and understood by the student. Even though the teacher is an expert in the subject area and has carefully prepared and effectively presented the material, these efforts still could be ineffective in the sense that the hearers do not act favorably to what they do hear and comprehend. In other words, often in the classroom there exists a *so-what* attitude. As outlined in Chapter 1, a very important step in the communication process is the listener's response, and without this step, all the other stages in the communication process are of little worth.

One of the purposes of higher education is altering or modifying behavior. Unless the student can be made to realize some good reason why he should learn certain subject material, and until he can be convinced of the relevancy of this information to his personal life and his interests and desires, he will resist filling his mind with "useless" knowledge. Just as it is necessary to awaken interest and capture the attention of the listener during the presentation of the subject matter for short-term effect, so likewise it is imperative for the teacher to generate intellectual excitement and provoke genuine motivation for long-term results.

Motivation may be defined as providing or assigning motives for desired behavior. It is part of the teacher's function to supply legitimate motives in order to stimulate learning. Motive appeals are appeals to feeling, needs, desires, ideals, sentiments or emotions. The effective teacher will learn how to vitalize these desires and needs of the students and associate these with the particular aims and purposes of the course. This, of course, implies that the teacher has had some acquaintance with educational psychology and remembers a sufficient amount of the undergraduate or graduate work in this area to be able to make the objectives of his subject matter appealing to the needs students have when they come to a college or university.

A good time to begin this motivational process is during the opening lecture, in clearly outlining the aims and purposes of the course, and also in describing the benefits each student can personally derive from a successful completion of the course when the objectives have been fulfilled. (Actually, before the student registers for the course, he should be motivated by the course description in the bulletin.)

One of the many courses I have taught is public speaking. Most students have a fear of getting up before the members of the class and delivering a speech, and I find that it is important that each student be highly motivated very early in the course. First of all, I review the probable motives which prompted them to go to college in the first place and then demonstrate how a public speaking class and speech training fulfills these goals and ideals. I endeavor to show how the information and training received in the course will fulfill the very desires and needs which prompted them to enroll in college. A brief review of the purpose of an overall college training as defined by Dr. Norvelle (*see* Chapter 1) is a good place to begin in this transfer of desires from that which the students have already declared, to those intrinsic in this particular segment of the curriculum. Norvelle's statement of the purpose of college training contains motivational elements "to gather subject material which will provide a background for needs after college and to develop habits which will enable the individual to adapt himself adequately to the cultural, social, economic, spiritual, and political demands of his generation."[1]

I try to show how speech training can accomplish or satisfy the aims of college training by helping them adequately to meet these various demands of their generation. Usually I begin with the *economic* demand and explain and illustrate how confidence, poise and the ability to communicate effectively can lead to success in whatever professional goal each one has envisioned. Some of the students may be planning on careers in chemistry, physics, engineering, nursing or medicine, but along with knowledge in these fields must be the ability to communicate and share this knowledge with other people. They will some day want to make others see things their way and convince others that their ideas and opinions are worth following. Skill in speaking is necessary to the college and university student's success, and has been considered by some as the greatest single success factor in determining how far one can go toward reaching a professional goal and the amount of time it will take to achieve such a goal.

Since speech is the chief means of expressing one's personality, and is an index to what we are and how we react to everything around us, any improvement in speech will be an improvement in one's social relations with others. Just as people quickly identify us *socially* by our speech, so they judge us *culturally* by the sound of our voice; what we say and how we say it.

Charles W. Eliot, noted educator and long-time president of Harvard University said, "I recognize but one mental acquisition as an essential part of the education of a lady or gentleman, namely an accurate and refined use of the mother tongue."

Skill in oral communication is of tremendous *political* consequence to the democratic way of life. The capable, civic-minded citizen cannot escape the necessity for effective public speaking. One of our basic obligations as citizens in a democracy is to guard the principle of free speech. One of the best ways to preserve this right is to exercise it.

From time to time during the course, some of these points are brought up again in an effort to keep the motivation levels high.

TYPES OF MOTIVATIONAL APPEALS

There will be no action or change of behavior unless there is strong motivation. A number of comparisons have been made to demonstrate the relationship and interdependence of the emotional and the logical in motivation. Logic is linked with information, but emotion is associated with action. Thought may construct the machinery, but feeling drives this machinery. Reason is like the arrow giving direction, but emotion is the force of the bow behind it.

In the older editions of his book, *Principles and Types of Speech*, Monroe cited four innate primary drives that prompt people into action: (1) Self-preservation and physical well-being; (2) preservation and increase in self-esteem; (3) freedom from restraints; and (4) preservation of the human race.[2]

In his book, *Motivation and Personality*, Maslow presents the following categories of needs and wants which impel human beings to think, act and respond as they do. Beginning at the bottom of his "pyramid of needs," he classifies them as *Physiological Needs* — food, drink, sleep, etc.; *Safety Needs* — security, stability, protection, freedom from fear and chaos; *Belonging and Love Needs* — acceptance and approval of family, friends and social groups; *Esteem Needs* — self-esteem from achievement, competence, confidence and recognition (status); *Self-Actualization* or *Self-Fulfillment* — to be what one can be and reach one's potential and capabilities.[3]

Among the strongest of the human feelings and most powerful emotions is love — love for God, country and family, all of which can lead to heroic actions, even the risking of one's own life. Fear of failure, guilt, pain and suffering, and fear of loss of security and life trigger strong action. Then there are other feelings, not as strong as the emotions of love and fear, such as pride, power, independence, savings, companionship, creativity and sympathy. Enjoyment of comfort and luxury, beauty and order, as well as pleasant sensations of taste, smell, etc. are personal desires with varying motivational force.

THE MOTIVATED SEQUENCE

It is essential to motivate students at the beginning of a course or occasionally to recapture this initial inspiration, but in addition a certain amount of motivation can be present in each daily lecture, or at least in certain problem-solving lectures. Monroe, who is so well-known for the psychological basis for speech organization referred to as the *Motivated Sequence*, developed an audience-centered approach to decision-making. The steps in this motivated sequence have been alluded to in the section of this book in connection with the inductive method of teaching. In order to get the audience involved and to prepare them for the final step of response or action, one must arrest the attention of his hearers. They must say, "I *want* to listen."

In order to sustain this initial interest, the teacher must quickly move into the second step — the *need step*, during which time he must involve students personally. They must be given an incentive for listening and must realize the need for the information which is being presented, so that each student says to himself, "This is important for me. I need to know this material. Something definite should be done about the situation." The teacher then leads them to take the third step — the *satisfaction step*, as he presents the solutions to the problem, answering important questions in the minds of the hearers, who then respond by saying, "I am glad that there are remedies to this problem." Just prior to the action step in the conclusion, the teacher should insert the *visualization step*, in which he presents either (or both) a negative, unfavorable result for the situation if one does not accept the remedy, or a positive, favorable condition if the solutions proposed are accepted. During this very important psychological step, each student visualizes himself in these contrasting situations, either of which could actually happen in the foreseeable future, and says, "I certainly don't want to experience the negative results, but greatly prefer to see myself in the rewarding positive circumstances." If each step thus far in the motivated sequence has been followed, the students will be adequately motivated to respond in the final *action step* by accepting the solutions suggested and saying, "I will do all I can to remedy this situation."

In order to involve the students in such a way so they will be led step by step as outlined previously, the teacher must first know the students and understand their general and specific desires and needs. Oliver stated

> A persuasive appeal acquires its motivational effectiveness by suggesting to the listeners that agreement with the speaker will satisfy their own needs, desires, and aspirations. In order to achieve this effect, the appeal gains strength by being aligned with their attitudes and by being presented in terms of their subjective interpretation of the subject. We find no reason to doubt that people can only be induced willingly to do what they desire to do.[4]

The teacher should be aware of any economical and social conditions, cultural attitudes and religious and political beliefs which might be peculiar among the members of the class. Appeals should be intelligently chosen. The motives must be relevant and not overdone and should be worthy of the response desired. Not all students are motivated by the same motive appeals, and the teacher should use a variety of appeals based upon a combination of feelings, wants and felt needs. Do not depend too heavily on the use of one strong appeal, such as fear, and do not overwork one appeal, especially fear. Coupled with fear can be sympathy, love and loyalty, etc. Today there is less emphasis on reliance upon rewards and punishments to develop motivation among students. There is, perhaps, a greater stress on social interaction, achievement and curiosity. People are naturally interested in knowing the *why* in casual relations. In contrast to the *fear of punishment* as a motivational factor is the *joy of discovery* and the excitement that can be derived from the satisfaction of *intellectual curiosity*. Commenting on this idealistic incentive, Jere W. Clark, in his article, "Creative Teaching," wrote

> Although agreeing that this is a fine ideal, most teachers in the past

have had little chance to approach or even little incentive to reach for it. The "born teacher" who had the rare combination of knowledge, personality, energy, ingenuity, and empathy could stir the curiosity of students with the use of few guidlines and special aids. Others were more or less forced by circumstances to fall back on methods less imaginative.[5]

These motives of intellectual curiosity, achievement and success are more effective and longer-lasting than the past method of conditioning and stimulus-response form of motivation. These threats of punishment and fear of failure may offer strong motivation, but often these are not long-lasting, although some type of reward, such as praise (not flattery) when rightly deserved and fairly meted out may be a justifiable mode of motivation. Bligh places great importance on praise:

> One of the most important things for a teacher to learn is to give praise. . . . Students may learn what they should *not* do by making mistakes; they learn what to do by the rewards of success. "Nothing breeds success like success" is a more pertinent dictum than "We learn by trial and error." To develop the drive to achieve, students need to believe that achievement is possible. This may be fostered if they can taste the fruits of success.[6]

Bligh added that positive feedback is a powerful motivator, and this is one important reason why there should be more opportunity given during lectures for student participation. Whatever the motives employed by the instructor, they must be consistent with logical thinking. True emotional appeals can legitimately and appropriately be used to reinforce the thoughts and concepts with vividness and power to activate responses. When motivational appeals are consistent with reason the effectiveness of classroom communication can be heightened.

The lack of motivation in the classroom is such a major breakdown in communication that it renders all other steps in the communication process as futile and useless. Without visible change of attitude and behavior the teacher's own motivation diminishes, and where no tangible student response can be noted, the task of teaching degenerates into frustration.

NOTES

1. Norvelle, Lee: Fundamental objectives of a teacher of speech in 1935. *Quarterly Journal of Speech, 21*:73, February, 1935.
2. Monroe, Alan: *Principles and Types of Speech,* 5th ed. Chicago, Scott, Foresman, 1962, p. 170.
3. Maslow, A.H.: *Motivation and Personality.* New York, Harpers, 1954, pp. 80-106.
4. Oliver, Robert T.: *The Psychology of Persuasive Speech,* 2nd ed. New York, Longmans, Green and Co., 1957, p. 48.
5. Clark, Jere W.: Creative teaching, *Improving College and University Teaching, 13, No. 2*:86, Spring, 1965.
6. Bligh, Donald A.: *What's the Use of Lectures?* Exeter Devon, published by D.A. and B. Bligh, 1971, p. 58.

Part IV
THE STUDENTS
Listening Skills and Feedback

CHAPTER 10

DEVELOPING LISTENING SKILLS

You must work extremely hard at listening. It is difficult
work, demanding concentration and knowledge of listening
techniques.

Monroe

WITHOUT the listener, communication does not exist in the classroom. The entire concern in this book and in the educational process itself is for the student. In all of the preceding chapters the responsibility for causing communication breakdowns in the classroom has been placed primarily on the teacher. It is true that the teacher and many aspects of teaching constitute the major reasons for these barriers. Some of the blame, however, must be shared by the students.

If the teacher is not sure of what he is saying and does not possess a pleasing personality; if the teacher lacks apparent dedication and the lectures are not well-organized and not adequately expressed in meaningful language and good style so that the students are unable to understand the verbal message (not to mention the nonexisting vocal and body messages); and if there is little to attract attention and develop interest, listening would be most difficult, and only the most hardy could survive because of extraordinary powers of concentration.

On the other hand, if the teacher really has something

worthwhile to say and possesses a dynamic or pleasing personality, acceptable to the listeners; if the students perceive the concern and dedication of their instructor, and if the lectures and discussions are well-organized, so that the listeners can determine the purpose and follow the unfolding of ideas which are adequately expressed in meaningful language and good style, so that the listeners can understand not only the verbal, but also the vocal and body messages; if the teacher captures the attention and creates interest in the students, then listening would indeed become a pleasure, or certainly much less difficult. Even if the teacher does a good job of presentation of the subject material, it is still possible for communication to break down because there is a lack of listening skills.

The students in the classroom are confronted with three messages being received simultaneously. Listening skills involve the student's ability to concentrate on the visual and aural messages and to decode and interpret them properly. Just as the production of speech through the operation of the mind and the vocal mechanisms in humans is a complex and astonishing accomplishment, so it is likewise with the listening process. Ehninger et al. wrote about this intricate process as follows:

> Listening is a complex psychological operation by which the bits and pieces of coded symobls and signals perceived by the central nervous system and the autonomic nervous system are converted into comprehensible messages . . . these bits and pieces are not those carried exclusively by words and sentences. A rasping voice, a vigorous gesture, tenseness of the facial muscles, a body still and slightly bent forward — all such stimuli are processed by your mind. . . . Thus listening, while principally an aural event, can involve almost all of your senses. It is, in short, the whole interpretative process whereby your body makes sense out of communicative stimuli.[1]

Even though this chapter deals with communication breakdown in *listening*, it actually includes seeing and perceiving, as well as interpreting all of the stimuli gathered by the senses. In the chapter dealing with attention and interest, the listener's extremely brief primary (complete) and even secondary (half-conscious) attention span was noted. It is difficult to keep the mind and sensory equipment or organs of perception fully concentrated on any one source of stimulus. The students are confronted, not only with external stimuli all vying for recognition, but internal stimuli, such as irrelevant thoughts competing with the teacher's presentation.

> Hearing — the psychological apprehension of aural stimuli — and listening — its psychological counterpart — are both highly complex processes which seem to guarantee that you seldom, if ever, will absorb, retain, and ultimately remember a speaker's message in all of its fullness and detail. As a result, you must work extremely hard at listening. It is difficult work, demanding concentration and a knowledge of listening techniques.[2]

As the students hear the actual word symbols as they are vocalized by the instructor, they must instantly understand and interpret each word or groups of words according to past experiences and associations they have had with these words. Second, the students must listen for the variations in the four aspects of vocal expression — rate, inflection, volume, and quality, and be sensitive to the different shades of meaning that they transmit. The third set of stimuli that makes up the total message involves the bodily movements and gestures which the student must observe at the same time while hearing and interpreting the words and vocal changes. These movements and gestures must likewise be comprehended and interpreted. All of these messages are fed into specialized areas in the cerebral cortex and cerebellum, which perceive and interpret in separate lobes auditory speech sounds and process visual symbols.

It is easy to see how a lack of listening technique constitutes one of the most serious breakdowns in classroom communication. The preceding chapters have outlined what the teacher can do to help the listener to avoid this barrier to attention and listening. What can the student do to minimize potential communication breakdown in listening? We are told that people remember only half of what they hear when tested immediately after listening, and remember only one-fourth after two months. Most people have formed very poor listening habits. We are constantly bombarded with sounds much of the day, such as people talking all around us either in person or via the radio and television (either ours or our neighbors). We cannot even shop in the supermarkets and department stores without being confronted with talking or music coming to us over the public address system. But even worse than all of this barrage of meaningful sounds of speech and music, everyone is daily subjected to unavoidable noises of transportation, construction, industry, and many other annoying babels of sounds and confusion. We have almost out of necessity, therefore, formed habits of allowing sounds to "go in one ear and out of the other ear," without concentrating on these stimuli. Attention or listening has become a matter of *selectivity*. In fact, some students (and older individuals) have *trained* themselves in such a way that they cannot apparently study without having music in the background. Radio and television often present news and other forms of information in brief, terse rapidly moving episodes, and television has conditioned the minds of young people to instantaneous images and pictorial presentations, so that when the students sit in class for fifty long minutes they find it almost impossible to concentrate on a sustained linear discourse.

LEVELS OF LISTENING

Ehninger, Monroe, and Gronbeck described three levels of hearing. All sounds travel by sound waves, which are transformed into auditory nerve impulses. Then these nerve impulses travel through the voluntary and involuntary nervous systems. The voluntary nervous system or the central nervous system processes messages which are directed to the *primary level* of hearing. These are messages which we think about, interpret and store in our minds. This is a voluntary response. The involuntary or autonomic nervous system works with the aural stimuli on the tertiary or involuntary response level of listening, as when we hear very loud noises and screams, and react involuntarily. In between these two levels of hearing is the *secondary level* in which we render only a half-conscious response as in the case of the student studying while half listening to background music.

Some of our listening is done with the purpose in mind of pure enjoyment, at which time we relax physically and mentally and just allow our thoughts and imagination to wander in accordance to whatever feelings might be evoked by the music or drama to which we have cultivated a receptive attitude. Listening for *understanding* or *comprehension*, however, is much more difficult, requiring the listener to assemble all of the facts being presented by the teacher. He reconstructs the speaker's outline, follows his line of reasoning, and compares the speaker's conclusion with his own beliefs and attitudes about the subject. The most difficult type of listening is the *evaluative listening*. The listener not only listens carefully to the major points or arguments, but he evaluates them critically and forms definite judgments concerning them.[3]

STUDENTS' THOUGHTS DURING LECTURES

Unfortunately, many students, even at the college and university levels, have not trained themselves for the latter two types of listening levels. In an effort to determine what thoughts go on in the minds of the students while the lecture or discussion is in progress, G. S. Bloom conducted a study a number of years ago, in which he used the *stimulated recall* method of reviving memories among the members of a class. By presenting certain stimuli that occurred in the original situation, the students relived their thoughts with vividness and accuracy. By exposure to certain sights, sounds or smells all of us have instantly recollected clearly some scene in our recent or far past which was associated with these visual, auditory, and olfactory stimuli. In Bloom's experiment, the entire class period lectures or discussions were recorded and soon after played back to the students, who were asked what they were thinking about when they originally heard each particular segment of the class period. The study included five lectures and twenty-nine discussions in social sciences, humanities and biological sciences. These thoughts were then classified into four general areas: (1) thoughts about other persons in the classroom, (2) thoughts about self, (3) irrelevant thoughts about persons, objects, and events not in the classroom, and irrelevant thoughts stemming from words and phrases used in the classroom, and (4) relevant thoughts about the subject itself, or application of subject material and attempts to find solutions or in evaluating the lecture or discussion. According to Bloom's studies almost one-third of the time during a lecture was spent in irrelevant thought.

There have been many articles written in which the authors declared that in the lecture, the students' role is a passive one, and since they are not under pressure to listen and are not threatened by being called upon to express their opinions or answer questions, their minds will wander from the subject matter being presented, much more than in a discussion. Bloom pointed out, however, that during a discussion there are many more opportunities for students' thoughts to be on other members of the class as they participate, than in a lecture where the thoughts are mainly on the lecturer. Also during a discussion students' thoughts will be on themselves to a much greater extent as they compare themselves with the other participants, or because of personal concerns of timidity and fear of saying the wrong thing and thereby displaying their ignorance. In one way it is easier to keep one's thought on the subject during the logically constructed arguments and well-ordered arrangement of subject material of a lecture than the generally less orderly and often inferior or inadequate student's comments as the teacher or leader tries to keep the discussion moving along on course. In discussion, according to Bloom, the student's thoughts are concerned with self almost one-fourth of the time as compared to 10 percent for lecturing.[4]

Ten years later a very similar study carried on at Miami University, Oxford, Ohio, was reported in the *Journal of Educational Psychology*. The same recall stimulus method was applied. After the lecture, a tape recording of it was played back and was stopped at each critical point, and the students were given two minutes to write down what they were thinking about at the point during the original presentation. Again in this study the thoughts were categorized into the two general classifications of irrelevant and relevant thoughts. While the teacher was talking one girl was thinking, "I wonder if John would ask me to go to the dance." Another student noted that the teacher was using a lot of *uhs* while he lectured. Other thoughts related to applying the subject material to their particular situation.[5]

TRAINING FOR GOOD LISTENING HABITS

In a chapter on "Two-Way Skills," Grambs, Carr, and Fitch declared that poor listening habits need retraining:

> More than any other skill, listening is taken for granted. It is assumed, somehow, that competence in recording and reacting to spoken

language develops on its own. The fact that students engage in listening more than in any other school activity may give rise to the idea that listening skills perfect themselves. Nothing could be farther from reality. . . . . Some situations encourage listening while others discourage it. . . . . Many students are not used to hearing intellectual conversation. Catching cue words, listening for the main idea, getting the sense of an involved statement — these are the problems of training.[5]

Just as the teacher must work hard to acquire good traits in class preparation and presentation, so the students must likewise sense their need to understand listening techniques and work diligently to acquire listening skills. Through lifelong acquisition of wrong habits of listening or plain lack of training or ignorance about correct listening principles, the learning process in higher education suffers greatly. We cannot take it for granted that good listening habits will be formed naturally in time.

It is difficult to pay full attention to the instructor when the student has not prepared for the class session through a careful study of the assignment. The teacher should encourage students to prepare for the following class by making definite assignments from the textbook and outside reading, and suggesting that the students look for the answers to specific questions or problems. Each student can develop an individual method for study, but should be acquainted with the technique of the *three S method*: *Scan*, in order to get the general idea of the lesson, such as the main points, theme or problems; *Study*, a careful reading of the assigned material, with an emphasis on the main points or answers to specific questions; and *Summarize*, just prior to class, or at least on the same day of the class, by reviewing the main points.

Once in class the student should determine to concentrate on the lecture or discussion, use willpower to keep irrelevant thoughts out of mind and put forth an effort to identify the structure of the outline or arrangments of the major ideas and subpoints being presented by the professor. A student should become discriminating in distinguishing the most important material from the relatively less important or insignificant subject matter. This will be most helpful in taking down notes that are meaningful. The more a student gets involved in the subject and the more he puts into listening, the more he will get out of the lecture or discussion. The student should note carefully how the professor elaborates on the information in the textbook, especially with the difficult sections of the lesson. The professor will probably clarify these points by definitions, illustrations, and possible demonstrations. Listening will become more meaningful if the student instantly interprets the denotation and connotation of words and the implications and emphasis conveyed through the teacher's voice, all of which is reinforced through bodily action.

In the case of discussions, the students must study the various viewpoints to be covered, come prepared to contribute on the different anticipated points and be ready to back up his comments and statements with appropriate evidence. Each discussant must develop the ability to analyze, evaluate, and relate the viewpoints of the others and learn to accept criticism of his own ideas. He does well to develop skill in tactful disagreement when this becomes necessary. Skills in listening, paying close attention and the ability to think clearly and quickly are most important in a teaching situation where discussion is the prime method employed.

OBJECTIVITY IN LISTENING

Undue bias and prejudice in the mind of the listener will cause communication to break down. There is no such thing as 100 percent objectivity. Everyone is biased, because each one has a set of beliefs and values, and tries to make everything fit into those views. When one is confronted with conflicting opinions the emotions may rise up and block out that which one does not want to hear. In order to become a good listener, one must learn to recognize these prejudices and attitudes or predispositions, and learn to control the emotions, so that they will not prevent a person from rational and logical thinking. A good listener will give the other viewpoints a fair consideration and allow time for evaluation. The students' biases may also be responsible for assumptions and inferences to be made which were not intended by the speaker.

Hearing is a normal bodily function, providing the hearing mechanism and nervous system are not impaired. Good listening, however, is not naturally acquired, but is something that needs to be, and which can be learned and improved. Listening is a skill that, like speaking, writing and reading involves the use, interpretation and evaluation of word symbols (and nonverbal cues). The proper listening skills will not make a good teacher out of a poor one, or transpose a dull lecture into an interesting one, but it can help to tolerate the more mediocre and even poor lecture or discussion period through greater powers of concentration, and it will help to identify, appreciate, and enjoy the rare masterpieces, as described by Frederick Mayer:

> A great lecture is as significant as a brilliant symphony. When it touches the hearts and the imagination of students it has a lasting value. . . . An inspired lecturer gives color to experience; he heightens the sensations of the moment.[7]

NOTES

1. Ehninger, Douglas, Monroe, Alan H., and Gronbeck, Bruce E.: *Principles and Types of Speech Communication,* 8th ed. Glenview, Scott, Foresman and Co., 1978, pp. 22, 23.
2. Ehninger, Douglas, et. al.: *Principles and Types of Speech Communication.* p. 24.
3. Ehninger, Douglas, et. al.: *Principles and Types of Speech Communication.* pp. 22-29.
4. Bloom, B.S.: Thought-processes in lectures and discussions. *Journal of General Education, 7:*163-165, October, 1952-July, 1953.
5. Siegel, Laurence, Siegel, Lila Corkland, Capretta, Patrick J., Jones, Reginald L., and Berkowitz, Howard: Students' thoughts during class. *Journal of Educational Psychology, 54, No. 1:*45-51, 1963.
6. Grambs, Jean Dresden, Carr, John C., and Fitch, Robert M.: *Modern Methods in Secondary Education,* 3rd ed. New York, Holt, Rinehart and Winston, Inc., 1958, pp. 98, 99.
7. Mayer, Frederick: Creative teaching, *Improving College and University Teaching. 8, No. 1:*42, Winter, 1960.

CHAPTER 11

STUDENT RESPONSE AND INTERPRETING FEEDBACK

Teaching is not a process, it is a developing emotional situation. It takes two to teach, and from all we know of great teachers the spur from the class to the teacher is as needful an element as the knowledge it elicits. In its most advanced phase, even the forbidden fault of thinking aloud becomes the most desirable product of the occasion.
Barzun

ONE of the greatest criticisms of the lecture method that is so often cited by the opponents of this technique is that it provides little, if any, interchange of thought or feedback between student and teacher. It is possible, of course, for this feedback to be lacking or to be inadequate in other methods of teaching, such as discussion, seminar and even tutorials. It is possible, however, to have feedback in the lecture, and this feedback need not all be oral, although there are no good reasons why a certain amount of oral feedback cannot be present during the lecture. It is not so much the nature of the teaching method of lecturing that is at fault in providing feedback, as it is the lecturer's unwillingness or hesitancy to provide opportunities for oral feedback or the professor's insensitivity to detect and interpret bodily reactions.

RESPONSE AND FEEDBACK

In the process of communicating in the classroom, the teacher is not only sending out messages constantly, but is also receiving messages constantly. Both the teacher and the students are sending and receiving messages at the same time. Any perceived message from the student is more accurately considered to be a *response*. When the student interprets what is heard, the reaction is an act of responding. *Feedback* is the receiver's messages sent in response to the source's messages. Strictly speaking feedback means that the person, who was the source of that which is being responded to, interprets the response.

Feedback can be positive or negative. In positive feedback, whether verbal or nonverbal, the receiver sends the message back to the source that the message is being received, understood, and accepted. Negative feedback (such as a frown or restlessness) is a message to the source that changes need to be made in the communication. A lack of response, or an absence of any observable response can, in fact, be interpreted by the source to mean a negative response.

There are a number of ways in which the students may express their reactions and attitude in a lecture. Facial expressions depict doubts, incomprehension, boredom, or interest, understanding, and even delight. Other bodily signs may indicate restlessness, loss of interest, etc.

TEACHER'S RESPONSIBILITY IN FEEDBACK

One cause of the problem is that many lecturers do not regard this matter of classroom feedback as their responsibility. Many who do consider feedback as desirable and even necessary to learning either do not know how to *read* and interpret it or do not actively work at studying ways to solicit and encourage student reaction. They may reason that, after all, higher education is a privilege open to a comparatively few individuals in a community or in society, and the student who is fortunate enough to be in a college or a university should realize this opportunity and make the best of it. The lecturer has spent many years in study and research and, perhaps, is sacrificing a much better paying position in business or industry, in order to make his or her expertise available to these favored few. Any teacher, however, who is not concerned with the students' individual needs and is unmindful of their reactions, or who does not provide adequate opportunities for feedback fails to perform the obligations and responsibilities in classroom communication.

In the book, *Classroom Behavior*, Mary Bany and Lois Johnson stressed the kind of relationship which must exist between teacher and students in a two-way communication system. "Communication is dual in nature. Teachers who succeed in achieving a general pattern of cooperative group behavior always develop two-way communication systems."[1] Students must be given opportunities to express themselves, so that mutual understanding is built between members of the class and the teacher. Effective teachers "are not only concerned with seeing that their messages are clear and received by the members of their classes; they are also attentive to the messages they receive."[2] The teacher must have the ability to receive as well as to send messages. Successful teachers consciously or unconsciously recognize that to help students learn — "whether the learning is in the area of skills or content or whether it pertains to attitudes and values," it is as important for the teacher to know what the students are saying as it is for the students to understand what the teacher is saying to them.[3]

Instead of the communication process comprising merely the passing of information from the teacher to the student it should be a dynamic interchange from the student to the teacher in which the teacher receives feedback as to how the messages are being received by the listeners so that the teacher can avoid belaboring the obvious and may sense the need of elaborating and elucidating material not fully comprehended by the hearers. There should be a continuous chain or loop of communication between teacher and student so that as the lecturer interprets this feedback he can make adequate *on the spot* revisions or further explanations and amplification, in an attempt to dissolve any misunderstanding or comprehension difficulties, all of which are constant potential breakdowns in communication.

Richard Startup commented on the importance of improvising

during a lecture as a result of the nonverbal as well as the verbal feedback:

> The feedback which was meaningful in a lecture context did not necessarily take verbal form. A lecture is essentially a dramaturgical production in which the lecturer may be able to survey the faces of his students and he may attempt to respond to the puzzlement or the interest or the amusement which he finds there. . . . The ability to improvise is important since unexpected or even bizarre events will impinge from time to time. A majority of the staff interviewed were conscious of demands made upon them. . . . They were aware, for instance that they needed a sense of timing.[4]

The forty-eight staff members who were interviewed in Startup's studies felt that it was desirable that feedback be received during the lecture, and three-quarters of them stated that they encouraged feedback, but most of them said that they did not receive a sufficient amount of feedback. Some of the lecturers felt that even if their words encouraged feedback, their manners did not, because it is not easy for a lecturer to be interrupted by questions from the students without giving the impression that these inquiries are indeed interruptions. Startup's studies also revealed that few lecturers seemed to have consciously developed strategies for encouraging feedback. Some of the lecturers, especially the inexperienced ones confessed that they "cling on to lecture notes" and "plough on regardless," even though they desired to give a "flexible performance." If some staff found "a lecture situation daunting," how intimidating must it be for some students to speak up in class before their fellow classmates and the professor.

THE ART OF QUESTIONING

One of the best ways to receive verbal feedback from the students is by asking questions. Questioning is a form of communication that requires a response. This can work both ways — questions that the professor asks the class or specific individuals, and questions that the members of the class ask the professor.

Lecturers often speak uninterruptedly for about forty minutes and then reserve the last ten minutes of class time for students to ask questions. But the danger with this method is that if no one asks any

questions, class is dismissed early, and thus a lack of feedback becomes a kind of *reward* for the students, and, generally, anyone who
raises questions at the close of the class period, while the others wish
to be dismissed can create a situation in which the questioner is de-
spised by his fellow classmates. Furthermore, if a student has a question at the beginning of the class period, he may either have
forgotten what the question was by the end of the lecture, or by that
time he may feel it was not important enough to forego early class
dismissal.

If the lecturer wishes to present material uninterruptedly, he can
lecture for ten or fifteen minutes until a specific segment of the subject matter has been covered and then stop the lecture and open up a
discussion period for five minutes or so. Startup found in his studies
that only a handful of staff sought to initiate discussion at regular in-
tervals during a lecture.

> There was general resistance to the idea that the audience should de-
> termine even a limited part of the course content. In practice, lecturers
> sought to restrict the number of exchanges, so that they could deal with
> a prepared range of topics. There can thus be seen to be tension between
> the lecturer's authority (expressed in his control over content) and his
> aim of making himself receptive to feedback.[5]

Bligh's studies indicated that questions are threatening stimuli
and produce a fear reaction.

> Using pulsimeters, I have found that the heart rate of students in a
> tutorial group increased by 5-10 beats per minute in the first 30 seconds
> after a tutor asked a question. The heart rate of students who spoke in-
> creased by 10-70 beats per minute. It seems reasonable to think that an-
> swering questions in the presence of a lecture audience would be an even
> more stressful situation. . . . I have found that students' heart rates rise
> appreciably when their neighbours speak.[6]

Bligh concluded that the questions themselves and the way they
are asked should be such as to produce minimal psychological stress.
In order to procure feedback from those students for whom this
public response is too stressful, the professor should use a less direct
method.

The nature of the subject matter, the disposition and educational
levels and maturity of the students and the experience and personality of the instructor may determine the type and extent as well as the
timing of questions during a lecture (or seminar and tutorial).

Encourage Students to Ask Questions

Not only should the professor address questions to the students in an attempt to gain some feedback from them (and to encourage them to study more diligently), but questions from the members of the class should be welcomed. Many lecturers give no opportunity for students to interrupt their lectures and to ask questions. In fact, some not only evade questions but seem annoyed by such intrusions and retaliate by reducing the question (or the questioner) to ridicule or even absurdity. Questions can be embarrassing to the teacher and can publicly demonstrate his ignorance in certain aspects of his discipline. Bluffing an answer is worse than admitting a lack of knowledge on a particular portion of the subject under discussion. If the lecturer is truly knowledgeable in his or her teaching field, and endeavors to keep up with the latest research in the discipline, there should be no apprehension or fear of being stumped by sincere student inquiry. In each class, the teacher might experiment to see which method of questioning would be most suited for that particular group: (1) brief discussion periods interspersed throughout the lecture or seminar, (2) at the end of the lecture, or (3) encouraging spontaneous questions anytime during the lecture at a point where a student may not comprehend what is being said, and at such times the student's experience or knowledge from his reading may prompt him to add some relevant information.

Guiding Principles in Asking Questions

There are a number of guiding principles or commonsense rules concerning the art of asking questions, eliciting answers, and answering student inquiries: (1) Ask sincere questions which relate to the students' interest and knowledge, and which are not too difficult. If the student does not seem to understand, the question might be rephrased. (2) Ask specific questions about material covered in class or textbook assignments. (3) Respect all responses and try to answer all questions satisfactorily before going on to another question. Admit lack of knowledge when necessary (and hope this will not have to happen too often)! (4) Involve other students beside the one asking the question, by inquiring what the others think about the point in question. (5) Ask *real* questions, not *canned* or artificial ones. On this matter Eble wrote:

> First, ask real questions even though they may seem offhand, simple, or imprecise. Nothing is more dismaying to the student than the canned question, of which the worst sort is the question picked up from a teacher's manual . . . and ill-suited to the teacher's own style. Such questions generally have canned answers, ones that the teacher alone knows and that students shoot at forever, scoring many near misses but never hitting the bull's eye. Moreover, such questions often are, or appear to be, invested with too much significance by the teacher. And worst of all, they are artificial.[7]

Dialogue Teaching

One excellent form of student involvement is the dialogical method of lecturing as opposed to the monological form. What is meant by dialogue in teaching? It is a conversation which the teacher has with himself or an imaginary person. Instead of the students asking the questions, the teacher asks the questions and searches for appropriate answers to these questions through the method of investigation. The inductive method of presentation mentioned in the chapter on organization can be adapted readily to the dialogue. Instead of giving the students the conclusion, the teacher presents the problem and then leads each student, as it were, individually through the entire process of investigation until suitable solutions are arrived at. In this way the student is forced to think for himself and to discover the answers, or, at least he is in some way involved, along with the others in the class, in a personal endeavor to search for the answers. In each step of the *thinking-it-through* process of anticipating questions and doubts or comprehending difficulties, the teacher is leading the individual student to participate, react and respond, or at least give some intellectual consideration to the problem or subject matter being presented.

The first step in presenting a problem dialogically would be to raise questions as to whether or not it is really a problem of sufficiently serious consequences to justify any real concern and consideration. The teacher now answers such inquiries by defining the problem or situation, explaining the implications and suggesting the possible ways it could affect everyday life. The next series of questions raised might relate to the reasons or causes for the existence of the present situation, in answer to which the professor can explore the possible causes and general background of the problem and also possibly give opportunity for the students to suggest other causes. As the dialogue continues in questioning what can be done to remedy the situation, the students are likely (audibly or in their own minds) to help suggest or think of solutions. The instructor might purposely offer "solutions" that would only aggravate the problem, and then, in the imaginary conversation, reject such suggestions, giving the reasons or citing the disadvantages, and, subsequently, offer alternative solutions. The teacher has two possible options — one is a conscious attempt through dialogue to lead the members of the class into a mutual agreement as to the best positive solutions, or with some problems demanding personal independent thought the final conclusions are left up to the individual students and need not necessarily be answered or suggested at the end of the lecture.

This dialogical method can effectively be employed in the formal or more informal lecture or act as an outline and give direction for movement in a discussion. Through asking questions and replying to his own questions, the lecturer is actually carrying out a debate with himself or with an imaginary opponent. This brings in the element of conflict, which not only stimulates interest but also teaches the principles of critical analytical thinking. Debate is essentially dialogical, asking significant questions, investigating possible solutions, and providing satisfactory answers based on valid evidence and sound reasoning.

All through this process, there is a two-way communication going on between the teacher and student, not necessarily an audible one, but rather a silent one. *Speaking* is (or should be) a matter of thinking out loud, and *thinking* is talking to oneself (in the mind of the listener).

Stolurow and Pahel referred to all effective teaching as an interaction between teacher and recipient, and, therefore, all good teaching is dialectic in nature:

> Teaching is fundamentally a social process involving communication and interaction between at least two people, a teacher and a student. It is a kind of dialectic in which both serve as teacher and student at different times and at different levels. A teacher is not only instructing a

student, but is also learning about that student and using what he learns in making decisions about what to do next in the course of teaching. Similarly the student is not only learning but is providing information to the teacher which in turn, guides the teacher in the ongoing interaction.[8]

STUDENT EVALUATION

Student evaluation through questionnaires constitutes another form of response, which the teacher should carefully observe and interpret and to which he or she should sensibly react. It is, however, only a *one-shot* student reaction and usually comes very late in the course when changes, at least for that particular class, would be quite unlikely. This feedback is very valuable (providing the professor is willing to face the facts about his teaching) to enable the teacher to see areas of weakness and communication breakdowns and give direction for specific improvement in further classroom interaction. Startup found it significant that only three of the forty-eight staff interviewed "attempted systematically to assess student reactions to their courses." From this situation, Startup concluded that "the widespread view that there was insufficient feedback appears to be a token acknowledgement of the need to assess performance through a consideration of 'consumer' reaction. It is hard to resist the conclusion that in the student interest much more systematic evaluation was required."[9] Bligh believed that "there may be a deep-rooted disinclination for the lecturer to face himself and his own performance."[10]

It is true that there are some objections to student evaluation of their teachers, as pointed out by Colin Flood Page in *Student Evaluation of Teaching*:

1. Students are not competent to judge the merit of either the process or the results of teaching.
2. It is a democratic fallacy that the teaching is best which pleases the majority.
3. Students are immature, superficial, mistaken and prejudiced. They are not only inclined to make snap judgements but in general their judgements are unreliable.
4. The validity and reliability of student judgement may be af-

fected and distorted by a variety of factors, among them grades, fondness or dislike for teachers, amount of work required by the teacher, the student's interest in the subject, and difficulty of the subject, etc.

5. Student ratings tend to disrupt the morale of the faculty. Student ratings may make the teacher too self-conscious for effective work, while low ratings may discourage him unduly.

6. Student ratings tend to have a disruptive effect on the morale of students, who feel they are the judges of the worth of teachers, curriculum and course content.

Colin Flood Page, however, enumerated more arguments for student evaluation of teaching than objections to these evaluations:

1. The educational process is, in essence, democratic, and the use of student opinion makes possible a wholesome kind of cooperative effort to improve the learning situation.

2. Any acceptable theory of learning stresses the importance of the learner's attitudes.

3. Students alone observe the teaching process day after day. The information acquired through systematic collection of their opinion is unique.

4. The views of the students may be prejudiced, mistaken, superficial, immature, but, whatever their validity, they exist and exert a powerful influence on the effectiveness of the course.

5. Analysis of student opinion often calls attention to undesirable attitudes, methods of instruction, courses of study, teacher personality, etc., of which teachers themselves are unaware.

6. Student opinion provides a quick, economical and easy means of evaluating teaching.

7. A rating program in which students participate tends to increase the interest of the teaching staff in teaching problems.[11]

If the daily lecture is truly a two-way communication situation, resulting in an abundance of student response, followed by immediate correct adjustment to feedback, the teacher need not fear students' written evaluation.

The inability of the teacher to produce favorable responses from the students, and the lack of skill in interpreting feedback constitute the most serious barriers to communication in the classroom. The

successful teacher is one who presents messages day by day worthy
of response, providing ample opportunities for such responses, and
interprets correctly and reacts wisely to the feedback. Joseph DeVito
expressed succinctly the importance and consequences of the teacher's role in feedback:

> Effectiveness in communication seems largely due to the ability of
> the communicator to respond appropriately to feedback. Teaching effec-
> tiveness may also be seen in the same way. Effective teachers seem to be
> those who can decode the responses of their students accurately and ad-
> just their messages accordingly. Ineffective teachers seem oblivious to
> how students are responding and just continue to communicate as al-
> ways.[12]

NOTES

1. Bany, Mary, and Johnson, Lois: *Classroom Behavior: Group Dynamics in Education.*
   London, Collier-Macmillan, Ltd., 1964, p. 109.
2. Bany, Mary, and Johnson, Lois: *Classroom Behavior: Group Dynamics in Education.*
   p. 109.
3. Bany, Mary, and Johnson, Lois: *Classroom Behavior: Group Dynamics in Education.*
   p. 109.
4. Startup, Richard: Staff experience of lectures and tutorials. *Studies in Higher
   Education, 2, No. 2*:193, 1979.
5. Startup, Richard: Staff experience of lectures and tutorials, p. 193.
6. Bligh, Donald A.: *What's the Use of Lectures?* Exeter, Exeter University;
   Published by D.A. and B. Bligh, 1971, p. 104.
7. Eble, Kenneth E.: *The Craft of Teaching.* San Francisco, Jossey-Bass Pub.,
   1976, pp. 59, 60.
8. Stolurow, L, and Pahel, K.: Letters to the editor, *Harvard Educational Review,*
   Summer, 1963, p. 384.
9. Startup, Richard: Staff experience of lectures and tutorials. p. 194.
10. Bligh Donald A.: *What's the Use of Lectures?* p. 109.
11. Page, Colin Flood: *Student Evaluation of Teaching: The American Experience.* Guild-
    ford, Society for Research into Higher Education, 1974, pp. 30-32.
12. DeVito, Joseph A.: *Communicology: An Introduction to the Study of Communication.*
    New York, Harper and Row, publishers, 1978, p. 16.

BIBLIOGRAPHY

Alciator, Robert T., and Alciator, Pegge L.: Consumer reaction to college teaching, *Improving College and University Teaching, 27, No. 2*:93-95, Spring, 1979.

Bandman, Bertram, and Guttchen, Robert S. (Eds.): *Philosophical Essays on Teaching.* Philadelphia, J.B. Lippincott Co., 1969.

Banks, Peter E.: Lecturing and all that, *Cambridge Journal of Education, 2, No. 1*:6-15, Lent, 1972.

Bany, Mary, and Johnson, Lois: *Classroom Behavior: Group Dynamics in Education.* London, Collier-Macmillan, Ltd., 1964.

Barzun, Jacques: *We Who Teach.* London, Victor Gollancz, Ltd., 1946.

Beard, R.M.: Bligh, D.A., and Harding, A.G.: *Society for Research into teaching methods in Higher Education,* 4th ed. Guildford, Research in Higher Education, 1978.

Berlo, David Kenneth: *Process of Communication: an Introduction to Theory and Practice.* New York, Holt, Rinehart and Winston, Inc., 1960.

Bligh, Donald A.: *What's the Use of Lectures?* Exeter, Devon, D.A. and B. Bligh Pub.: University Teaching Methods Unit, 1971.

Bligh, Donald A.: Ebrahim, G.M.: Jaques, David, and Piper, D. Warren. *Teaching Students.* Devon, Exeter University Teaching Services, 1975.

Bloom, B.S.: Thought-processes in lectures and discussions, *Journal of General Education, 7*:160-169, October, 1952-July, 1953.

Bonhorst, Ben A.: The scholar-teacher, *Improving College and University Teaching, 7, No. 1*:41-44, Winter, 1959.

Bowman, James S.: The lecture-discussion format revisited, *Improving College and University Teaching, 7, No. 1*:25-27, Winter, 1979.

Bradford, Leland P.: The teacher in the learning group, *Improving College and University Teaching, 27*:99-103, 1959.

Brembeck, Winston L., and Howell, William, S.: *Persuasion --A Means of Social Control.* New York, Prentice-Hall, 1952. (See Chapter XV, Attention)

Clark, G. Kitson, and Clark, E. Bidder: *The Art of Lecturing.* Cambridge, W. Heffer and Sons, Ltd., 1959.

Clark, Jere W.: Creative teaching, *Improving College and University Teaching, 13, No. 2*:86-88, Spring, 1965.

Coats, William D., and Smidchens, Uldis: Audience recall as a function of speaker dynamism, *Journal of Educational Psychology, 57, No. 4*:189-191, August 1966.

Cockburn, Barbara, and Ross, Alec: *Lecturecraft.* Lancaster, University of Lancaster, 1977.

Collier, K.G.: An experiment in university teaching, *Universities Quarterly, 20*: 336, June 1966.

Conant, James Bryant: *The Education of American Teachers.* New York, McGraw-Hill Book Co., 1963.

Cooper, B., and Foy, J.M.: Evaluating the effectiveness of lectures, *Universities Quarterly, 21, No. 2*:182-185, March, 1967.

Cross, K. Patricia: *The Instructional Revolution.* Paper presented at Concurrent General Session I, 31st National Conference on Higher Education, sponsored by American Association for Higher Education, Chicago, Monday, March 8, 1976.

D'Angelo, Edward: Classroom emotional experiences, *Improving College and University Teaching, 19*:329-330, 1971.

DeVito, Joseph A.: *Communicology: An Introduction to the Study of Communication.* New York, Harper and Row Publishers, 1978.

Doob, Leonard W.: *Propaganda.* New York, Henry Holt and Co., 1935.

Eble, Kenneth: *Professors as Teachers.* San Francisco, Jossey-Bass Pub., 1972.

_____: *The Craft of Teaching.* San Francisco, Jossey-Bass Pub., 1976.

Ehninger, Douglas, Monroe, Alan H., and Gronbeck, Bruce E.: *Principles and Types of Speech Communication,* 8th ed. Glenview, Scott, Foresman and Co., 1978.

Ellis, H.P., and Jones, A.D.: Anxiety about lecturing, *Universities Quarterly, 29*:91-95, Winter, 1974.

Fessenden, Seth A.: Johnson, Roy Ivan, and Larson, P. Merville: *The Teacher Speaks.* New York, Prentice-Hall, Inc., 1954.

Flesch, Rudolf: *The Art of Readable Writing.* New York, Harper and Brothers, 1949.

French, Florence: *Radio English.* New York, McGraw-Hill, 1952.

Fuller, James A.: What's wrong with our higher education? *Improving College and University Teaching, 13, No. 2*:120-121, Spring, 1965.

Furedy, Chris: Improving lecturing in higher education, *The Canadian Journal of Higher Education, 9, No. 1*:45-54, 1979.

Gage, N.L. (Ed.): *Handbook of Research on Teaching.* Chicago, Rand McNally and Co., 1963. Chapter XI, Getzels, J.W. and Jackson, P.W.: The teacher's personality and characteristics.

_____: *The Psychology of Teaching Methods.* Chicago, The National Society for the Study of Education, 1976.

Garrison, Roger H.: What's the message? *Improving College and University Teaching,*

13, No. 2:91-93, Spring, 1965.

Glicksberg, Charles I.: Is lecturing teaching? *Improving College and University Teaching, 6, No. 1*:26-29, Winter, 1958.

_____: What makes a classroom? *Improving College and University Teaching, 5, No. 2*:69-73, 1957.

Grambs, Jean Dresden: Carr, John C., and Fitch, Robert M.: *Modern Methods in Secondary Education*, 3rd ed. New York, Holt, Rinehart and Winston, Inc., 1958.

Gregory, I.D.: A new look at the lecture method, *British Journal of Educational Technology, 6, No. 1*:55-62, 1975.

Hale, Sir Edward, Chairman: *Report of the Committee on University Teaching Methods*. London, Her Majesty's Stationary Office, 1964.

Hatch, Winslow R.: The "dialog", *Improving College and University Teaching, 6, No. 3*:73-74, 1958.

_____: When students play on the team, *Improving College and University Teaching, 2*:49-50, 1958.

Hayakawa, S.I.: *Language in Thought and Action*. London, George Allen and Unwin, Ltd., 1952.

Henderson, Norman K.: *University Teaching*. Hong Kong, Hong Kong University Press, (through Oxford University Press), 1969.

Heslet, Frederick E.: Communication pragmatics of the lecture, *Improving College and University Teaching, 19*:190-191, 1971.

Highet, Gilbert: *The Art of Teaching*. London, Methuen and Co., Ltd., 1951. (Reprint 1963).

Hills, Philip: *Teaching and Learning as a Communication Process*. London, Croom Helm, Ltd., 1979.

Hough, Richard: *Mountbatten, Hero of our Time*. London, Weidenfeld and Nicholson, 1980.

Jackson, David, and Jaques, David: *Improving Teaching in Higher Education*. London, University Teaching Methods Unit, 1976.

James, William, *Psychology*. New York, H. Holt and Co., 1904.

Jefferson, Charles Edward: *The Minister as Prophet*. New York, Gosset and Dunlap. 1905, quoting Charles Eliot.

Johnstone, A.H., and Percival, F.: Attention breaks in lectures, *Education in Chemistry, 13, No. 2*:49-50, March, 1976.

Kelly, Brenda Wright, and Homes, Janis: The guided lecture procedure, *Journal of Reading, 22, No. 7*:602-604, April, 1979.

King, Margaret: The anxieties of university teachers, *Universities Quarterly, 28*:69-83, Winter, 1973.

Kyle, Bruce: In defense of the lecture, *Improving College and University Teaching, 20*:325, 1972.

Layton, David (Ed.): *University Teaching in Transition*. Edinburgh, Oliver and Boyd, 1968. (Fitzgerald, P.J.: The lecture: an arts view, pp. 11-17, Laing A.: The art of Lecturing, pp. 18-34, and Wise, Arthur: Talking to large groups, pp. 35-43).

Lee, Calvin B.T. (Ed.): *Improving College Teaching.* Washington, American Council on Education, 1967, (quoting Wise, Max: Who teaches the teachers? pp. 77-89.)

Lee, Irving J.: *Language Habits in Human Affairs.* New York, Harper and Brothers, 1941.

Lloyd, D.H.: Communication in the university lecture, *University of Reading Staff Journal, No. 1*:14-22, February, 1967.

Lucio, William H. (Ed.): *Readings in American Education.* Chicago, Scott, Foresman and Co., 1963.

McFarland, H.S.N.: *Intelligent Teaching.* London, Routledge and Kegan Paul, 1973.

McKeachie, Wilbert: Research on teaching at the college and university level. In Gage, N.L. (Ed.) *Handbook of Research on Teaching.* Chicago, Rand McNally and Co., 1963, pp. 1118-1173.

_____: Procedures and techniques of teaching: a survey of experimental studies. In Sandford N. (Ed.) *The American College.* New York, Wiley, 1962.

McLeish, John: *The Lecture Method.* Cambridge, Institute of Education (Heffers of Cambridge), 1968.

MacManaway, L.A.: Using lecture scripts, *The Universities Quarterly, 22*:327-336, June, 1969.

Marshall, Max S.: Is it interesting? *Improving College and University Teaching, 21, No. 1*:17-18, 1973.

Maslow, A.H.: *Motivation and Personality.* New York, Harpers, 1954.

Matthews, T.H.: The training of university teachers, *The Universities Quarterly, 5, No. 3*:269-274, May, 1951.

Mayer, Frederick: Creative teaching, *Improving College and University Teaching, 8, No. 1*:41-47, Winter, 1960.

Milton, Ohmer, and Shoben, Edward Joseph (Ed.): *Learning and the Professors.* Athens, Ohio University Press, 1968, quoting Hutchinson, William R. (also found in *Improving College and University Teaching, 17*:107, 1969.

Mollet, David: Students' evaluation of teaching methods and changes in teaching methods, *Assessment in Higher Education, 2, No. 2*:135-155, February, 1977.

Monroe, Alan: *Principles and Types of Speech,* 4th ed. Chicago, Scott, Foresman, 1955. (also 6th ed. Glenview, Scott, Foresman and Co., 1967).

Morton, Richard K.: Education as free communication, *Improving College and University Teaching, 19*:220, 1971.

_____: Learning as communication, *Improving College and University Teaching, 19*:143-145, 1971.

_____: Personal backgrounds of effective teaching, *Improving College and University Teaching, 8*:136-137, 1960.

Mouly, George J.: *Psychology of Effective Teaching,* 2nd ed. London, Holt, Rinehart and Winston; a Holt International Edition, 1970.

Norvelle, Lee: Fundamental objectives of a teacher of speech in 1935, *Quarterly Journal of Speech, 21*:73, February, 1935.

Oliver, Robert T.: *The Psychology of Persuasive Speech,* 2nd ed. New York, Longmans,

Green and Co., 1957.

O'Neill, James Milton, and Weaver, Andrew Thomas: *Elements of Speech*. (rev. ed.) New York, Longmans, 1933.

Page, Colin Flood: *Student Evaluation of Teaching: the American Experience*. Guildford, Society for Research into Higher Education, 1974.

Palzer, Edward: Professorial speech blockage, *Improving College and University Teaching*, 7:89-93, 1959.

Peters, R.S. (Ed.): *John Dewey Reconsidered*. London, Routledge and Kegan Paul, 1977.

Phillips, Arthur E.: *Effective Speaking*. Chicago, The Newton Co., 1938.

Powell, Len: *Lecturing*. London, Pitman Pub., 1973.

Quintilian: *The Institution Oratoria of Quintilian*, xi, iii, trans. Butler, H.E. New York, G.P. Putnam's Sons, 1922.

Rees, Richard: Dimensions of students' points of view in rating college teachers, *Journal of Educational Psychology*, 60: pp. 476-482, 1969.

Report of Commission on Teaching in Higher Education, Presented to Liverpool Conference, April, 1969. London, National Union of Students.

The Robbins Committee Report on Higher Education. Appendix Two (B) London, Her Majesty's Stationary Office, 1963.

Rothwell, C. Easton, Chairman: *The Importance of Teaching*, Report of the Committee on Undergraduate Teaching. 1st Printing June, 1968. 7th Printing, May, 1973. New Haven, The Hazen Foundation.

Rovin, Sheldon, Lalonde, Es effectivenessrnest, and Haley, John H.: An assessment of the lecture, *Improving College and University Teaching*, 20:326, 327, Autumn, 1972.

Rowland, Ray: Can teaching be measured objectively? *Improving College and University Teaching*, 18, No. 2:153-157, Spring, 1970.

Rudin, Stanley A., Measuring the teacher's effectiveness as a lecturer, *Journal of Genetic Psychology*, 98: pp. 147-154, 1961.

Ryan, T. Antoinette: Research: guide for teaching improvement, *Improving College and University Teaching*, 17:270-276, Autumn, 1969.

Ryckman, Richard M.: *Theories of Personality*. New York, D. Van Nostrant Co., 1978.

Sala, John R.: Dialog teaching, *Improving College and University Teaching, 13, No. 2*:94-96, Spring, 1965.

Salomon, Louis B.: *Semantics and Common Sense*. New York, Holt, Rinehart, and Winston, Inc., 1966.

Setterfield, George: Elements of creativity in teaching. In Sheffield, Edward F. (Ed.): *Teaching in the Universities: No One Way*. Montreal, McGill-Queen's University Press, 1974, pp. 43-53.

Sarett, Lew, and Foster, William Trufant: *Basic Principles of Speech*. Boston, Houghton Mifflin Co., 1936.

Schwartz, Lita Lizer: Criteria for effective university teaching, *Improving College and University Teaching*, 28, No. 3:120-123, 1980.

Scott, Walter Dill: *Psychology of Public Speaking*. New York, Noble and Noble

Publishers, 1926.

Shannon, Claude, and Weaver, Warren: *The Mathematical Theory of Communication.* Urbana, University of Illinois Press, 1959.

Sheffield, Edward F. (Ed.): *Teaching in the Universities: No one Way.* Montreal, McGill-Queen's University Press, 1974.

Siegel, Laurence, Siegel, Lila Corkland, Capretta, Patrick J., Jones, Reginald L. and Berkowitz, Howard: Students' thoughts during class: a criterion for educational research, *Journal of Educational Psychology, 54, No. 1*:45-51, 1963.

Smelser, Neil J., and Smelser, William T.: *Personality and Social Systems.* New York, John Wiley and Sons, Inc., 1963.

Smith, Henry Clay: Team work in the college class, *The Journal of Educational Psychology, 46, No. 5*:274-286, May, 1955.

Startup, Richard: Staff experience of lectures and tutorials, *Studies in Higher Education, 2, No. 2*:191-201, 1977.

Stolurow, L, and Pahel K., Letters to the editor, *Harvard Educational Review, Summer, 1963.*

A student forum, Improving College and University Teaching, 17:162-163, 1969. (editorial) (quoting Tyson, Stephen E.)

Süsskind, Charles: On teaching science teachers to teach, *Improving College and University Teaching, 5, No. 1*:46-48, Winter, 1957.

A talking teacher cannot succeed, *Improving College and University Teaching, 7, No. 2*:67, 1959. (editorial)

Tead, Ordway: The evaluative point of view, *Improving College and University Teaching, 8, No. 1*:4-10, Winter, 1960.

_____: Twelve suggestions for improving teaching, *Improving College and University Teaching, 6, No. 2*:105-106, 1958.

Thompson, Ralph: Legitimate lecturing, *Improving College and University Teaching, 22*:163-164, 1974.

Thonssen, Lester, and Baird, A. Craig: *Speech Criticism.* New York, Ronald Press, 1948. (also 2nd ed 1970)

Travers, Robert M.W.: *Second Handbook of Research on Teaching.* Chicago, Rand McNally and Co., 1973. Trent, James W., and Cohen, Arthur M.: Research on teaching in higher education. pp. 1034-1041.

Trott, J.R.: Lectures, lecturers, and the lectured. *Improving College and University Teaching, 11, No. 2*:72-75, Spring, 1963.

Ullmann, Stephen: Words with Blurred edges. In Anderson, Wallace L., and Stageberg, Norman C. (Eds.): *Introductory Readings in Language.* Rev. ed. New York, Holt, Rinehart and Winston, 1966.

Warga, Richard G.: *A Psychology of Personal Adjustment,* 2nd ed. Boston, Houghton-Mifflin Co., 1979. (See Chapter 1, quoting Allport).

Wiedmann, Paul, and Dorward, Neil: Education in economics: an evaluation of the mass lecture as a teaching technique in first-year economics, *Economics, 8, Part 4, No. 60*:110-111, Winter, 1977.

Wilkinson, Andres, Stratta, Leslie, and Dudley, Peter: *The Quality of Listening.* New York, Macmillan, 1974.

Williams, Reed G., and Ware, John E., Jr.: Validity of student ratings of instruction under different incentive conditions: a further study of the Dr. Fox effect, *Journal of Educational Psychology, 68, No. 1*:48-56, 1976.

Wilson, John F., and Arnold, Carroll C.: *Public Speaking as a Liberal Art,* 2nd ed. Boston, Allyn and Bacon, Inc., 1968.

Winans, James Albert: *Public Speaking.* New York, The Century Co., 1917.

Wise, Arthur: Talking to large groups. In Layton, David (Ed.): *University Teaching in Transition.* Edinburgh, Oliver and Boyd, 1968, pp. 35-43.

Wise, Max: Who teaches the teachers? In Lee, Calvin B.T. (Ed.): *Improving College Teaching.* Washington, D.C.: American Council on Education, 1967, pp. 77-89.

Wolf, Dan B.: Can education learn from business? *Improving College and University Teaching, 13, No. 2*:110-111, Spring, 1965.

INDEX